THE DESI RETIREMENT PLAN

A Practical Framework for a
Worry-Free Retirement in India.

Includes the **Desi Retirement Preparedness Score (DRPS)**

SURAJ KAELEY

notionpress.com

INDIA • SINGAPORE • MALAYSIA

ISBN
Paperback 979-8-90431-356-2
Hardcase 979-8-90431-930-4

Contents

PART - III

BUILDING A RESILIENT RETIREMENT PORTFOLIO

PART - IV

THE DESI INVESTMENT PRODUCTS

PART - V

MAXIMISING YOUR RETIREMENT YEARS

Acknowledgements

Writing "The Desi Retirement Plan" has been a deeply fulfilling journey; one that would not have been possible without the support, encouragement, and contributions of a few incredibly special people.

First, I would like to thank my wife, Rashmi. Her unwavering belief in me, her patience through the long and often demanding writing process, and her constant encouragement have been the emotional foundation of this book.

I would like to express my heartfelt gratitude to Maneesha and Gopal Vaidyanathan. Their involvement in this book has been truly exceptional. They went through the manuscript page by page, offering thoughtful, practical, and often incisive feedback. Their insights helped sharpen the ideas, improve the structure, and ensure that the content remains relevant and relatable. This book is significantly better because of their generous contribution of time and effort.

To my son, Sparsh, thank you for your curiosity and fresh perspective. Your questions encouraged me to simplify complex ideas and communicate them more clearly.

To my daughter, Shivani, I am deeply grateful for your meticulous editing and keen eye for detail. Your ability to refine my thoughts and present them in a more structured and reader-friendly manner has added immense value to this book.

Finally, to my readers, thank you for placing your trust in me. My sincere hope is that this book helps you take charge of your retirement with clarity, confidence, and purpose.

Introduction

Ajay Banerjee, a successful head of marketing with a multinational company, was waiting for his flight at Mumbai airport. He was glued to the announcements being made, and as soon as the announcer mentioned his flight number, he knew his flight would be delayed. Now he had almost three hours to kill.

He walked over to the bookshop, and a book on retirement planning immediately caught his attention. Like most Indians, he had never really given adequate thought to this subject. It was always on his mind—one of those things he would get to "someday". Here was a God-sent opportunity to finally do it. He bought the book, found a quiet corner near his gate, and started reading.

The book was American. The author was confident. The message was simple: "Retirement planning is easy. You need 25 times your annual expenses as your retirement corpus. Just start with a withdrawal rate of 4% per year, adjust withdrawals for inflation every year, and you're set for 30 years."

Ajay pulled out his phone and opened the calculator app. His current monthly expenses: ₹80,000. That's ₹9,60,000 per year. Twenty-five times that: ₹2.40 crores.

He had ₹1.8 crores already. Just 60 more lakhs to go, and according to this book, he'd be ready for retirement. He should have felt relieved. Instead, he felt uneasy. Something did not add up.

He looked up from the book and stared at the departure board. His mind wasn't on the flight anymore.

It was on his father. His father was 78, living in Kolkata. Still independent, still sharp, but the medical bills were climbing. ₹15,000 per month now for medicines alone. Ajay had been covering it for the past three years. How long would that continue? Another 10 years? 15? The book didn't mention supporting parents.

Then there was his daughter. Priya was 22, working at a startup in Bangalore. Good job, but the salary was modest. She'd been dropping hints about wanting to do an MBA—preferably abroad. That's at least ₹50 lakhs. And after that? Marriage. Everyone would expect him to contribute at least ₹30 lakhs, probably more, given his position. The book didn't mention funding children's aspirations.

His son, Arjun, was 20, in his third year of engineering. Bright kid, but he wanted to go to the US for his master's. Another ₹60 lakhs, minimum. Ajay hadn't said no because how could he? He'd worked this hard so his children could have opportunities he never did. The book didn't mention that either.

Then there were the smaller things. His younger brother, who had been struggling with his printing business for years. Every few months, there was a "temporary cash flow issue." Ajay always helped. What was he supposed to do—say no?

The annual trips to Kolkata for Durga Puja. The expected gifts for his nephews and nieces. The contributions whenever someone in the extended family faced a crisis. The temple donations that his mother insisted on. The family gatherings he was supposed to host.

None of it was large individually. But collectively? The book didn't mention any of it.

And then there was the biggest uncertainty: his own career. He was 52. His company had just gone through a restructuring. "Rightsizing," they called it. He'd survived this round, but for how long? Two years? Five? The new CEO was 38 and kept talking about "fresh thinking" and "digital transformation." What if he didn't make it to 60? What if there were a VRS next year?

The book assumed he'd work until he chose to retire. That's not how corporate India works.

Ajay closed the book and set it on the seat beside him. The math was simple. The assumptions were neat. The promise was seductive.

BUT NONE OF IT FIT HIS LIFE.

The book said he needed ₹2.4 crore to cover his ₹80,000 monthly expenses. But his actual expenses weren't ₹80,000. When he included everything—his father's support, the amortised cost of his children's upcoming needs, the family obligations, the cultural expectations—his real monthly outflow was closer to ₹1,40,000.

That wasn't ₹2.4 crores. That was ₹4.2 crores. And he had ₹1.8 crores. The gap was ₹2.4 crores—exactly what the book said he needed in total. He wasn't even close.

But here's what troubled him most: the book treated retirement as if it were just about him. As if he could isolate his financial life from his family's. As if obligations, relationships, and culture didn't matter. As if retirement were a solo sport.

That's not retirement in India. That's not his life.

Ajay looked at his phone, then back at the book. The book had no answers for this.

The announcement came: his flight was now boarding. Ajay picked up the book, walked to the gate, but his mind was searching for answers. He didn't need a book written for someone else's retirement. He needed a plan for his own.

A plan that acknowledged his father would need more support as he aged, not less. A plan that accounted for his children's futures without bankrupting his own. A plan that made room for family obligations without apology or guilt. A plan that worked, even if his corporate career ended earlier than expected.

HE NEEDED A PLAN FOR *DESI* RETIREMENT.

Not the American 4% rule. Not the neat assumptions. Not the fantasy of retiring in isolation. Western retirement planning assumes you retire at 65 with a paid-off house, zero dependents, government healthcare, and social security. Your only job? Manage your money and play golf. That's not your retirement.

YOUR RETIREMENT IS MESSIER. MORE COMPLICATED. MORE INDIAN.

It's not just about you. It's about your parents who need you. Your children who aren't quite independent yet. Your extended family who looks up to you as the "successful one." The cultural obligations you can't escape. The relationships that matter more than any spreadsheet.

Western retirement planning gives you a number.

DESI RETIREMENT DEMANDS A FRAMEWORK—ONE THAT FITS YOUR LIFE, NOT SOMEONE ELSE'S FANTASY.

Ajay is not alone! Thousands of Indians in their 50s—successful, disciplined, hardworking—sitting on large retirement corpuses feel the same way. They read the same books, use the same calculators, follow the same advice. But none of it works for them. They continue to search for answers and need reassurance that in the end, all will be well.

Because Indian retirement isn't about a number; it's about an ecosystem. It's about parents and children and siblings and culture and obligations and relationships that matter more than any spreadsheet.

The math is the easy part. The reality is what's complicated.

This is Why This Book Exists. It helps you think through the challenge of managing your finances in retirement in a simple, structured, step-by-step manner so that you can lead a worry-free retirement life. And, more importantly, it is written with the Indian context in mind.

I'm Suraj Kaeley. I'm 60 years old. I've spent over three decades in India's financial services sector with some of the largest asset management and insurance firms—Franklin Templeton, MetLife, Fidelity, and UTI Asset Management.

Seven years ago, I had the same questions as Ajay. As I sat down to plan my retirement, confident that my career in finance had prepared me. I had the knowledge. I had the discipline. I had the savings. What I didn't have was a framework that fit my life.

Every retirement planning model I knew was built for western retirees. Most of them solo retirees. Retirees with no parents to support, no children needing help, no extended family obligations, no cultural expectations. That wasn't my retirement. And it's not yours either.

I have spent the last five years creating a framework that works for Indian families. I realised that all of us are looking for answers to some simple questions:

- Will my money last?
- Where should I invest my retirement corpus?
- How do I deal with medical emergencies?
- How would I deal with a market meltdown or a COVID-like situation?
- Am I being selfish for not helping more?
- What if I live to 90 or 100?
- Can I afford to retire, or do I have to keep working?

And through this book, I am happy to share with you "The Desi Retirement Plan"—a framework that acknowledges the reality Ajay faced that day at the airport.

This book won't tell you retirement planning is simple. It's not—not for us. But it will give you something better than simplicity: Clarity.

Clarity about who you are planning for.

Clarity about what your real expenses are—not just yours, but your circle's.

Clarity about how much you need.

Clarity about how to balance helping your family with protecting your own future.

And most importantly: clarity about whether your money will last your lifetime.

WHAT'S IN THIS BOOK?

PART I: UNDERSTANDING DESI RETIREMENT

Why western retirement planning fails Indian families, the six fatal mistakes most people make, and a quick reflection on where you stand today from a retirement perspective.

PART II: BUILDING YOUR DESI RETIREMENT PLAN

The Desi Retirement Plan consists of six sections, starting with naming everyone in your core circle and your promises to them. In Section 2, you will calculate your real expenses, prepare for medical emergencies, and assess the impact of inflation on your expenses. Section 3 is focused on the income sources and the retirement corpus that can help us fund our expenses. Section 4 helps you assess your retirement preparedness with the help of a single number—Annual Withdrawal Rate (AWR). Next, you will figure out how you can improve your retirement preparedness. Sections 5 and 6 deal with investing your retirement corpus and legacy planning, respectively. These sections are discussed in detail in Parts III, IV, and V of the book.

PART III: BUILDING A RESILIENT RETIREMENT PORTFOLIO

Investing is a big part of a retirement plan. In this part, we focus on all the aspects from an investment standpoint. You will learn about asset classes and asset allocation, keeping retirement in mind. You will be able to identify your investment biases and learn how you can get over them to create a genuinely diversified portfolio that not only has the potential to beat inflation but also reduces the volatility substantially. You will learn how to build a portfolio robust enough to navigate major market downturns, a portfolio that keeps taxation in mind—all discussed with minimal use of jargon. You will also do a stress test by relaxing some of the assumptions. so that you are better prepared to deal with situations you do not normally expect in your retirement years.

PART IV: THE DESI RETIREMENT PRODUCTS

In this section, I have discussed products relevant from a retirement income standpoint. I have discussed the SLRT Framework so that you can assess all products in a consistent and comprehensive manner. Next, I have discussed products that can provide predictable income—Bank FDs, GOI Bonds, Tax-Free and Taxable Bonds, and Annuities. You also need products that have the potential to provide a higher income and tax efficiency. Mutual Funds, REITs, and InvITs are helpful in that regard. You will learn more about these products and how to use them appropriately in your investment portfolio.

PART V: MAXIMISING YOUR RETIREMENT YEARS

This part starts with legacy planning. What you can do to ensure that your wealth and legacy pass on seamlessly to your rightful successors. We also discuss the relevance of Active Income and Regular Savings in your retirement years. I have dedicated a chapter to women investors and discussed the specifics they need to focus on from a retirement perspective.

The book concludes with an assessment tool titled The **Desi Retirement Preparedness Score (DRPS)** that will help you assess at a granular level your retirement preparedness on all dimensions of the retirement plan.

WHO SHOULD READ THIS BOOK?

This book is for you if:

You're in the age bracket of late 40s to early 60s, thinking actively about your retirement and wondering if you're ready.

You want a plan that's honest about the complexity without drowning you in it.

You need confidence—not just about your corpus size, but about your ability to navigate 30 years of retirement with dignity and independence.

A PROMISE AND A WARNING

The Promise: By the end of this book, you'll have a complete Desi Retirement Plan that fits your life—one you can review quickly, adjust when life changes, and follow with confidence in your retirement years.

The Warning: This book won't tell you that everything will be easy. Your retirement will involve difficult choices—helping family versus protecting your corpus, working longer versus retiring sooner, supporting parents versus leaving more for children.

I won't make those choices for you.

But I'll give you a framework to make them thoughtfully, with full awareness of the consequences, and without the regret that comes from decisions made in confusion.

Turn the page, and let's build your Desi Retirement Plan—one that works for your life, your family, and your future.

PART - I

UNDERSTANDING DESI RETIREMENT

1

What Does "Retirement" Mean to You?

Retirement is often seen as the final goal of your working life. Work hard for many years, save enough money, and then finally stop working. The popular image of retirement is simple—relaxed mornings, travel plans, time with family, and freedom from deadlines and pressure. For many people, this idea is comforting and even motivating.

But the truth is that retirement is not a single event or a fixed destination. It is a long phase of life, and the way you choose to live it can be very different from how someone else chooses to live theirs. Two people with the same savings and similar backgrounds can experience retirement very differently. One may feel peaceful and in control, while the other may feel restless and anxious. The difference is often not money alone; it is the mindset.

Before thinking about numbers, investments, or plans, it is important to pause and ask a simple but powerful question:

"What does retirement really mean to you?"

THE TWO EXTREMES OF RETIREMENT THINKING

Most people think about retirement in one of two extreme ways, often without realising it.

At one end is the idea that retirement is a time to stop doing anything productive and simply enjoy life. At the other end is the belief that one should continue working exactly as before and never really retire at all. Both views are common, and each comes with its own risks.

Understanding these extremes is important because your financial decisions are influenced by how you see your retirement years.

THE "DO NOTHING" VIEW OF RETIREMENT

For many people, retirement means freedom from routine. No alarms, no meetings, no targets, and no pressure. After decades of hard work, the desire to slow down and rest is natural. In fact, taking time off to relax and recharge is healthy and necessary.

Problems begin when rest becomes the only plan.

After the first few months, many retirees find that too much free time creates its own challenges. Days lose structure. Physical activity reduces. Mental engagement drops. Social interactions slowly decline. Over time, this can affect not just emotional health, but physical health as well.

Doing nothing sounds peaceful. Living without purpose rarely is.

THE "KEEP WORKING" VIEW OF RETIREMENT

At the other extreme are people who believe retirement does not apply to them. They see work as a source of identity, confidence, and relevance, and they want to continue for as long as possible. This thinking is common among professionals, entrepreneurs, and senior corporate executives.

There are clear benefits to this approach. Staying engaged in meaningful work keeps the mind active and often brings a strong sense of satisfaction. Continued income also reduces pressure on retirement savings and provides flexibility in spending and investing.

But this approach carries its own assumptions, and that is where the risk lies.

It assumes that health will always cooperate, that skills will remain relevant, and that opportunities will continue to exist. Industries change, technology advances, and client expectations evolve. Many people who plan to work "as long as they want" eventually discover that the decision is no longer entirely in their hands.

Planning to work forever is not a plan. It is a hope.

A "BALANCED APPROACH" TO RETIREMENT

Somewhere between the two extremes is the balanced approach to retirement.

They decide not to work at the same pace as before, but at the same time, they have enough and more time to devote to themselves and their families. They want to feel useful, relevant, and independent.

This balanced approach fits naturally into Indian life. Family responsibilities continue well into later years. Children may need support. Parents may need care. Social and cultural expectations remain. At the same time, people want control over their time and energy.

This is where a balanced approach to retirement makes sense. Some years may be more active, others slower. Income may continue in different forms—part-time work, advisory roles, small business involvement, or project-based assignments. The goal is not to maximise income, but to preserve flexibility and purpose.

RETIREMENT DOES NOT MEAN STOPPING. IT MEANS CHOOSING.

Why These Choice Matters Financially?

Your philosophy of retirement has a direct impact on your finances.

If you plan to stop working completely, your savings must last longer and absorb more shocks. If you assume you will always earn, you may underestimate the need for safety and stability. A balanced approach allows room for adjustment when life changes.

Retirement in India can easily last 30 years or more. During this time, inflation will rise, healthcare costs will increase, and markets will go through multiple cycles. A rigid mindset makes these challenges harder to manage. A flexible mindset makes them easier to handle.

Money lasts longer when your thinking is flexible.

A WORD OF CAUTION

There is a lot of noise around retirement today. Early retirement stories, financial freedom movements, and social media images often create unrealistic expectations. Doing nothing forever or retiring very early may sound attractive, but without a clear idea of how you will spend your time and stay engaged, these ideas can lose their appeal quickly.

Retirement is not about escaping work; it is about deciding how you want to live a life that is satisfying and meaningful to you.

SETTING THE FOUNDATION

This book focuses on helping you build a practical, realistic financial framework for retirement, tailored to Indian families and realities. But no framework can work well unless it is aligned with how you want to live your life.

There is no single correct way to retire. What matters is that your financial decisions support your chosen way of living, not fight against it.

In the next chapter, we will look at the **six fatal mistakes** people make while planning for retirement. These mistakes are common, avoidable, and often expensive. Understanding them early will help you make better choices as you move forward.

Every good plan starts with clear thinking. This chapter was about thinking clearly. Let's move ahead.

2

The Six Fatal Mistakes That Destroy Desi Retirement Plans

In the previous chapter, we explored three fundamental approaches to retirement: doing nothing, continuing to work, or a more balanced approach that combines leisure with purpose. Whichever path you choose, one truth remains universal: your retirement plan must be built on solid foundations.

Yet even the most disciplined, successful individuals often discover too late that their retirement plans were constructed on faulty assumptions. Not because they lacked intelligence or diligence, but because they were following frameworks designed for someone else's reality.

This chapter identifies the six most common mistakes that destroy desi retirement plans. Each one is preventable. Each one is addressed in the Desi Retirement Plan framework. But first, you need to see them clearly.

MISTAKE #1: FOCUSING ONLY ON SELF - NOT EVEN INCLUDING YOUR SPOUSE

The most fundamental error in retirement planning is also the most common: calculating based on your expenses alone.

Most retirement books ask: "How much are you likely to spend each month in your retirement years?" As Ajay did, you guess your monthly expenses, multiply by 12, apply the 25x rule, and arrive at an amount that would last your lifetime. Simple. Except it's dangerously incomplete.

The question isn't "What do I spend on?"

THE QUESTION IS "WHO DEPENDS ON ME FINANCIALLY?"

For most Indians, that list is longer than they initially acknowledge. Your spouse—whose expenses might differ from yours and whose longevity might exceed yours by 5 to 10 years. Your ageing parents who need monthly support that increases as medical needs grow. Your children who reach financial independence later than previous generations—after expensive education, marriage, perhaps a down payment on their first home. Your extended family, where being the "successful one" comes with unstated but very real financial obligations. The cultural expectations that aren't optional—festivals, family gatherings, contributions to relatives' life events.

When you account for your actual desi circle, the number often grows by 50% to 100%.

THAT'S NOT A SMALL MISCALCULATION.

The fix begins with honest accounting. Write down every person whose financial life touches yours. Quantify the support you currently provide and reasonably expect to provide over the next 20 to 30 years. Include the lumpy expenses—weddings, education, medical emergencies, and loan repayments—these could be infrequent but are large enough to easily derail your retirement plan. The number will be larger than you want it to be. But it will be real. And only real numbers lead to plans that work.

MISTAKE #2: UNDERESTIMATING LONGEVITY - YOURS AND THEIRS

Most people still plan for a 20-year retirement. That assumption is increasingly dangerous.

Life expectancy in India, particularly for educated urban professionals with access to good healthcare, is approaching 90–95 years. If you retire at 60, you're not planning for 20 years. You're planning for 30, possibly 35 years. That's not a minor adjustment—it could increase your required corpus by 50% to 75%.

When you retire at 60, your parents are likely to be 80–85 years old. They could easily live another 10–15 years. That's a decade or more of support during which their medical costs don't decrease—they multiply. What costs ₹15,000 per month today becomes ₹40,000 per month as they require more intensive care, medications, and assistance.

And the uncomfortable truth is that the longer your parents live, the older you become. By the time you're managing their end-of-life care at age 95, you're 70 yourself. Your earning capacity is zero. Your own healthcare costs are climbing. You're caught in a financial squeeze at precisely the moment you have the least flexibility to manage it.

When you plan for 20 years, you calculate one corpus requirement. When you plan for 30–35 years of your own retirement plus extended parental support, the required corpus often doubles. Planning for age 85 feels conservative. Planning for age 90 is a realistic exercise in prudence.

If you plan for 95 and die at 85, your children inherit extra money. If you plan for 80 and live to 95, you become a burden. Which risk would you rather take?

MISTAKE #3: FAILING TO ACCOUNT FOR REAL INFLATION

Everyone includes inflation in their retirement calculations. The problem is they use the wrong number.

The RBI publishes general inflation at 5%–6%. So, most retirement plans assume 5% inflation across all expenses for the next 30 years. This is mathematically neat and catastrophically wrong.

Inflation isn't uniform for all of us. The number that you pick should reflect your personal reality. Let me share a couple of examples. If you are not in reasonable health and have a significant healthcare expense, the inflation could be as high as 7%–8% for you. Education costs inflate at 8%–10% if you're contributing to your children's advanced degrees. Wedding expenses inflate at 8%–12% as social expectations rise, and venue costs explode. Even cultural and social obligations inflate at 6%–8%.

A 1% estimation error in inflation rates can hurt you badly. A 2% error will certainly derail the best of plans.

At 5% inflation, your ₹50,000 monthly expense becomes ₹2,16,000 in 30 years. At 7% inflation, it becomes ₹3,80,000—76% higher. That's not a rounding error. That's the difference between having enough money and running out at age 80.

The fix requires calculating your specific effective inflation rate based on your actual expense mix, then using that number—not the general inflation rate—in your projections. It means separating high-inflation expenses, like healthcare, from low-inflation expenses, like groceries, because averages obscure reality. The numbers get worse when you do this honestly. But honest numbers are the only ones that lead to adequate planning.

MISTAKE #4: RELYING ONLY ON HEALTH INSURANCE FOR MEDICAL EXPENSES

Health insurance is essential. Health insurance is also insufficient.

Most people buy adequate coverage—₹10 lakhs, ₹25 lakhs, even ₹50 lakhs, and assume healthcare costs are handled. Then reality arrives in the form of hospital bills.

The hospital bill says ₹4 lakhs. Your insurance pays ₹2 lakhs. You pay ₹2 lakhs out of pocket. Why? Room rent exceeded the policy cap; a proportionate deduction was applied. Consumables not covered—gloves, syringes, bandages add up. Co-payment clause—you pay 20% of everything. Certain medicines not on the approved list—denied. Effectively, the insurance covered 50%, while you thought it covered 100%.

Then come the expenses that insurance doesn't touch at all. The medicines your parent takes every month—₹15,000 worth of monthly prescriptions. Insurance coverage: zero. It's OPD, not hospitalisation. The quarterly diagnostic tests, the regular doctor visits, the physiotherapy sessions—all essential, all expensive, all uncovered.

Over a 20-year retirement, if total healthcare costs for your circle average ₹6 lakhs annually and insurance covers 30%–40% of that, you're paying ₹4 lakhs per year out of pocket. That's ₹80 lakhs over 20 years, ₹1.6 crores over 30 years—from your retirement corpus, not from insurance.

And here's the desi reality: you're not just planning for your healthcare. You're planning for your parents', possibly your in-laws', and sometimes contributing to your children's medical needs. Healthcare expenses aren't individual line items. They're family system costs.

The solution isn't just buying more insurance, though better coverage helps. It's creating a three-layer defence: adequate insurance with proper coverage terms, a dedicated healthcare fund, separate from your retirement corpus, to cover gaps and emergencies, and immediate liquidity access for hospital deposits before insurance processes claims. Each layer catches what the previous layer misses. Together, they prevent medical costs from destroying your retirement plan.

MISTAKE #5: BUILDING A SKEWED PORTFOLIO INSTEAD OF A HOLISTIC ONE

Most people think they have diversified portfolios. They have mutual funds, some FDs, maybe some stocks, and perhaps some gold. "Well diversified," they tell themselves.

Then you look more closely and discover that 60% of the equity portion is held in one company's stock from ESOPs. Or 80% of the portfolio is in fixed deposits earning 6.5% while inflation runs at 6%–7%. Or ₹50 lakhs are locked in PPF and real estate with zero liquidity when flexibility is desperately needed. Or taxes consume 25%–30% of returns, turning an apparent 8% return into an actual 5.5% post-tax return.

These aren't diversified portfolios. These are product collections with dangerous concentrations, return blindness, liquidity mismatches, and tax inefficiency.

Concentration risk means too much in one company, one sector, one asset class, or one illiquid investment. If your company struggles, your employment and your portfolio crash simultaneously. If the banking sector corrects, your "diversified" equity holdings will all fall together because they're concentrated in a single sector.

Return blindness means looking at nominal returns without accounting for inflation or taxes. An FD earning 7% sounds safe until you realise inflation is 6% and you're in the 30% tax bracket. Your real, post-tax return is a negative 1.1% (7% tax adjusted @30% tax rate is 4.9% less inflation of 6% = -1.1%). Over 30 years, that difference of 1.1% destroys purchasing power by almost 40%. And you then start to withdraw from your principal amount to meet your expenses. The net result: you run out of money when you need it the most!

Liquidity mismatch means money is locked when you need flexibility. That commercial property worth ₹50 lakhs generates zero income when vacant and takes months to sell in an emergency. That

₹35 lakhs in PPF are wonderful for safety, but useless when you need ₹10 lakhs immediately for your parents' surgery.

Tax inefficiency means failing to structure investments to minimise tax drag. Earning ₹15 lakhs annually sounds good until taxes reduce it to ₹12 lakhs. That 20% difference means you need 20% more corpus to generate the same post-tax income.

Building a holistic portfolio means honest assessment of concentration risks, understanding real returns after inflation and taxes, maintaining appropriate liquidity for your life stage, considering tax efficiency in product selection, and having the discipline to rebalance when allocations drift. It means thinking about your portfolio as an integrated system, not a collection of individual products.

MISTAKE #6: NOT HAVING AN ESTATE PLAN

Estate planning feels like something to do "later." You're only 52, 55, 58—plenty of time, right?

Then your colleague dies suddenly at 56. Healthy one day, massive heart attack the next. His ₹2.3 crore estate—spread across eight banks, four brokerages, three mutual fund houses—became a nightmare for his family. No updated nominations. No will. Investments scattered in his name, his wife's name, and joint names. The legal process to settle: three years and counting. Family access to funds during that time: minimal. Legal fees: ₹8 lakhs and rising.

Your family needs money immediately when you die. Daily expenses don't stop. Medical emergencies don't pause. Children's education can't wait. But without proper estate planning, your money gets locked in probate proceedings for years.

Worse, estate planning in desi families isn't just about spouse and children. It's about dependent parents you're supporting, commitments to extended family, cultural expectations about inheritance, and multiple generations with potential claims. Without clear documentation, your death creates financial chaos and family conflict at the worst possible moment.

The fix isn't complicated—make a will with clear asset distribution, update all nominations across every financial account, create a simple folder with account details and access information, have a clear conversation with your spouse about money and obligations, and review it annually. One weekend of work could save your family years of legal battles and emotional trauma.

THE PATTERN BEHIND THE MISTAKES

These six mistakes share a common origin: they come from using western retirement planning frameworks for the desi retirement reality.

Western planning assumes you're planning for yourself, perhaps a spouse. Desi reality means planning for an extended circle.

Western planning assumes 3% inflation. Desi reality shows 6%–8% effective inflation, varying wildly by category.

Western planning assumes insurance handles healthcare. Desi reality shows insurance covering 30%–40%, with you paying the rest.

Western planning assumes diversification is automatic. Desi reality requires active portfolio construction and discipline. Western planning assumes simple estate distribution. Desi reality involves complex multi-generational obligations.

These aren't minor adjustments. These are fundamental differences that require a different framework entirely.

The good news: once you see these mistakes clearly, they're preventable. Each one has solutions. Each one is addressed systematically in the Desi Retirement Plan framework.

I have given a broad context in which retirement planning has to be done. Now it's time to focus on your retirement plan.

In the next chapter, you will start by reflecting on where you stand today. Do not be surprised if you are committing some of these fatal mistakes. Do not worry; you will be able to correct them as you go ahead.

3

Where Do You Stand Today?

You know the six fatal mistakes that destroy retirement plans. You understand why western frameworks don't work for desi retirement. You know that your retirement corpus must support not just you, but an entire ecosystem of relationships and obligations.

Now comes the most important question: Where do you stand today?

Most people avoid this question. They have a vague sense of their financial situation—"I have some mutual funds," "My PF balance is decent," "I own some property"—but they've never actually sat down and taken complete stock. It's like trying to plan a journey without knowing your starting point. You might have a destination in mind, but without knowing where you are, you can't chart the route.

Before you build your Desi Retirement Plan, you need a clear snapshot of your current reality—not what you think you have, not what you hope you have, but what you have today, right now, in concrete numbers.

This isn't about precision down to the last rupee. This is about honest awareness. Where are you in your life? Where are you financially? How much time do you have to bridge any gaps? These answers determine everything that follows.

So, before we dive into defining your circle, quantifying expenses, or calculating corpus requirements, we start with the simplest but most essential step: understanding exactly where you stand today.

YOUR CURRENT POSITION: FOUR QUESTIONS

Take out a piece of paper or open a simple spreadsheet. You're going to answer four questions. Don't overthink them. Don't try to be precise. Round numbers are fine. The goal is clarity, not perfection.

QUESTION 1: HOW MUCH TIME DO YOU HAVE?

Write down three numbers:

Your current age: _____

Your planned retirement age: _____

Years remaining until retirement: _____

If you're 52 and planning to retire at 60, you have 8 years. If you're 55 and could potentially work until 65, you have 10 years—but be realistic about whether you'll make it that long given VRS trends, industry changes, or your own health and energy.

This number—years remaining—is crucial. It determines how much more you can save, how much your existing corpus can grow, and how aggressive or conservative you need to be with your planning. Someone with 10 years has options someone with 2 years doesn't have. Know which situation you're in.

QUESTION 2: WHAT ARE YOU EARNING TODAY?

Write down your current annual income from all sources:

Salary/professional income: ₹_____

Rental income: ₹_____

Business income: ₹_____

Other income: ₹_____

Total annual income: ₹_____

This tells you your current earning power and your capacity to save between now and retirement. If you're earning ₹20 lakhs annually and can save ₹5 lakhs per year, that's ₹40 lakhs more corpus over 8 years, plus growth. If you're earning ₹8 lakhs and barely breaking even, you won't be able to close gaps through additional savings—you'll need to adjust the plan itself.

QUESTION 3: WHAT DO YOU HAVE TODAY?

Now comes the slightly harder part: tallying up your current assets. Don't log into every account. Don't check today's NAV. Use approximations based on your last statement or your best recollection. You're looking for a ballpark total, not an audit.

List your assets by category:

Your debt will include your bank deposits, PF, PPF, Bonds, debt mutual funds, and investments in arbitrage or equity savings funds.

Your equity will include stocks, equity mutual funds, private equity, PMS, and AIF. Include your investments in hybrid funds like Balanced Advantage or Multi-Asset funds here.

Gold and precious metals include physical gold (coins, gold bars) but exclude jewellery for personal use. You can add Gold/Silver ETFs, Sovereign Gold bonds here.

If you own real estate other than the house you live in, the same will be included here. You will estimate it at 80% of its value to account for any taxation or loss in market value in the future.

The easiest way to fill this section is to generate your e-CAS statement from the NSDL or CDSL website. The e-CAS statement lists all your investments made in the capital markets. These include stocks, PMS, AIF, mutual funds, Bonds, NPS… everything. The only things missing here are your bank deposits and insurance policies.

Notice what we're NOT including: your primary residence. The house you live in is not part of your retirement corpus unless you plan to monetise it by selling and downsizing or taking a reverse mortgage. For now, exclude it. Also, exclude any business assets if you own a business—those require separate valuation and liquidity analysis.

What you're calculating is your liquid or near-liquid investible wealth—the money that can fund your retirement expenses. This is the summary of your total investments.

Debt Investments: ₹_______

Equity Investments: ₹________

Precious Metals (excluding jewellery): ₹_______

Real estate (excluding primary residence): ₹_______

Total investible assets: ₹__________

Now that you know your total investible assets, do you think they would be adequate to retire on? Is there any skew towards any of the categories? When you were listing your assets, did you notice any concentration? These are the kinds of questions we need to ask and make the necessary changes.

QUESTION 4: WHAT ARE YOU SPENDING TODAY?

This is often the trickiest question because most people don't track their expenses. They have a rough sense—"Maybe ₹60,000 a month", but when you add up rent or EMI, utilities, groceries, help at home, transportation, entertainment, dining out, medical costs, insurance premiums, children's expenses, support to parents, festival spending, and miscellaneous everything-else, the number is usually 30%–50% higher than the initial guess.

For now, make your best estimate:

Monthly household expenses: ₹_____

Annual expenses: ₹_____ (monthly × 12)

If you have old credit card statements, bank statements, or any expense-tracking records, use them. If not, estimate conservatively. It's better to overestimate expenses than underestimate them.

And here's a critical note: this is just your baseline household expenses today. In the next section of the book, you'll break this down in much greater detail, add in your circle's expenses, account for major one-time costs, and factor in inflation. For now, you just need a rough current number.

Your Starting Point Snapshot

Now you have four key numbers in front of you:

Years to retirement: _______

Current annual income: ₹_______

Current total assets: ₹_______

Current annual expenses: ₹_______

These four numbers don't tell you if you're ready to retire—that comes later when you build your complete framework. But they tell you what kind of situation you're starting from: comfortable, manageable, or crisis. And that determines how you'll approach every subsequent step.

WHAT THESE NUMBERS REVEAL

Your four numbers paint a picture. Not the complete picture—that requires the full Desi Retirement Plan framework—but an initial sketch that tells you something important about your readiness.

If you have 8–10+ years until retirement: You have time. Time to save more, time to let your corpus grow, time to adjust, time to course-correct if things aren't working. This is your advantage. Use it. Don't waste these years assuming you'll "figure it out later." Later has a way of arriving faster than you expect.

If you have 2–4 years until retirement: Time is short. Your runway is almost over. You need clarity immediately. You need to know if you're ready or if you need to delay retirement, reduce expenses, or dramatically increase savings. This isn't about perfection—it's about realistic assessment and decisive action.

If you're already retired or within a year of retirement: Your numbers are essentially locked. What you have is what you have. Your focus shifts from accumulation to management—making what you have last, optimising withdrawal strategies, and managing risk carefully. The framework still applies, but your options for major changes are limited.

If your current assets are 25–30x your annual expenses: You're probably in a strong position. A corpus of ₹2.5 crores supporting ₹10 lakh annual expenses gives you a 4% withdrawal rate starting point. You are in a good situation if there are no other major expenses to fund from this corpus.

If your current assets are 10–15x your annual expenses: You're in the zone of concern. A corpus of ₹1.5 crore supporting ₹12 lakh in annual expenses implies an 8% withdrawal rate. That's high. Sustainable for maybe 10–15 years, but risky for a 30-year retirement. You need to either increase corpus, reduce expenses, or plan for ongoing income in retirement.

If your current assets are less than 10x your annual expenses: You're in crisis territory. A corpus of ₹1 crore supporting ₹12 lakh annual expenses means a 12% withdrawal rate. That's not a retirement plan—that's a countdown to running out of money. You need immediate, aggressive action: delay retirement significantly, cut expenses dramatically, or plan to work through retirement. There's no gentle way to say this—the math doesn't work.

These are rough heuristics, not final verdicts. Your actual retirement readiness depends on factors we haven't analysed yet—your desi circle obligations, inflation, healthcare costs, investment allocation, and expected returns. But these initial ratios tell you whether you're starting from a position of strength, adequacy, or crisis.

WHAT TO DO WITH THIS INFORMATION?

You now have your starting point documented. Don't judge it. Don't panic if the numbers aren't where you hoped they'd be. Don't become complacent if they look better than you expected. Just acknowledge the reality.

Write these four numbers somewhere you can refer to them easily—at the top of your worksheet, in a dedicated notebook, in a simple spreadsheet. These are your baseline numbers—everything that follows builds on them.

Here's what will happen in the next section of this book: your expenses will expand as you consider your full desi circle—parents, children, extended family, cultural obligations, healthcare, and major life events. The ₹10 lakh or ₹15 lakh annual expense number you wrote down today will likely grow to ₹18 lakhs, ₹22 lakhs, or even higher. This isn't about becoming extravagant; this is about being honest about who you're supporting and what they'll need.

Your required corpus will increase accordingly. And you'll need to confront whether what you have is genuinely adequate or whether gaps exist that need closing.

But you can't confront what you can't see. And now you can see where you stand today.

In Part II of this book, we'll build your complete Desi Retirement Plan—step by step, element by element. We'll define your circle, quantify every expense, account for inflation, build a healthcare defence, identify income sources, inventory investments properly, and calculate your true retirement readiness.

But all that starts here, with these four simple numbers you've just written down. You know where you stand today.

PART - II

BUILDING YOUR DESI RETIREMENT PLAN

4

Introducing the Desi Retirement Plan

In this chapter, I will introduce the Desi Retirement Plan Framework. A practical, step-by-step framework designed for how Indians live, earn, spend, and support their families. This framework will become the backbone of your retirement planning.

This is not just another financial exercise. This is a pause. A moment of honesty. A conversation with yourself about the life you want to live, and the responsibilities you will continue to carry.

Retirement, as we often imagine it, is not a neat milestone—a date, a number, a finish line. In my view, it is a journey, and all you are doing here is building a roadmap that helps you track your progress in your retirement years.

THE DESI RETIREMENT PLAN IS STRUCTURED AROUND SIX SECTIONS.

Each one addresses a distinct dimension of your retirement. Together, they form a complete picture not just of your finances, but of your life in retirement.

Section 1: People & Promises: Who are you planning for, and what have you promised them?

Section 2: Lifestyle & Risks: What will your retirement life cost, and what could derail it?

Section 3: Income Sources & Retirement Corpus: How will you fund your expenses? How much money do you have available to fund your retirement?

Section 4: Your Retirement Preparedness: Will your money last your retirement years? And if not, what will you do about it?

Section 5: Optimising Your Investment Portfolio for Retirement: Are you carrying biases that could hurt you in retirement? Is it positioned to handle any eventuality that may arise?

Section 6: Passing on the Legacy: What happens after you?

The Desi Retirement Plan template is available at the end of the chapter. Here is a schematic diagram to help you visualise the Desi Retirement Plan.

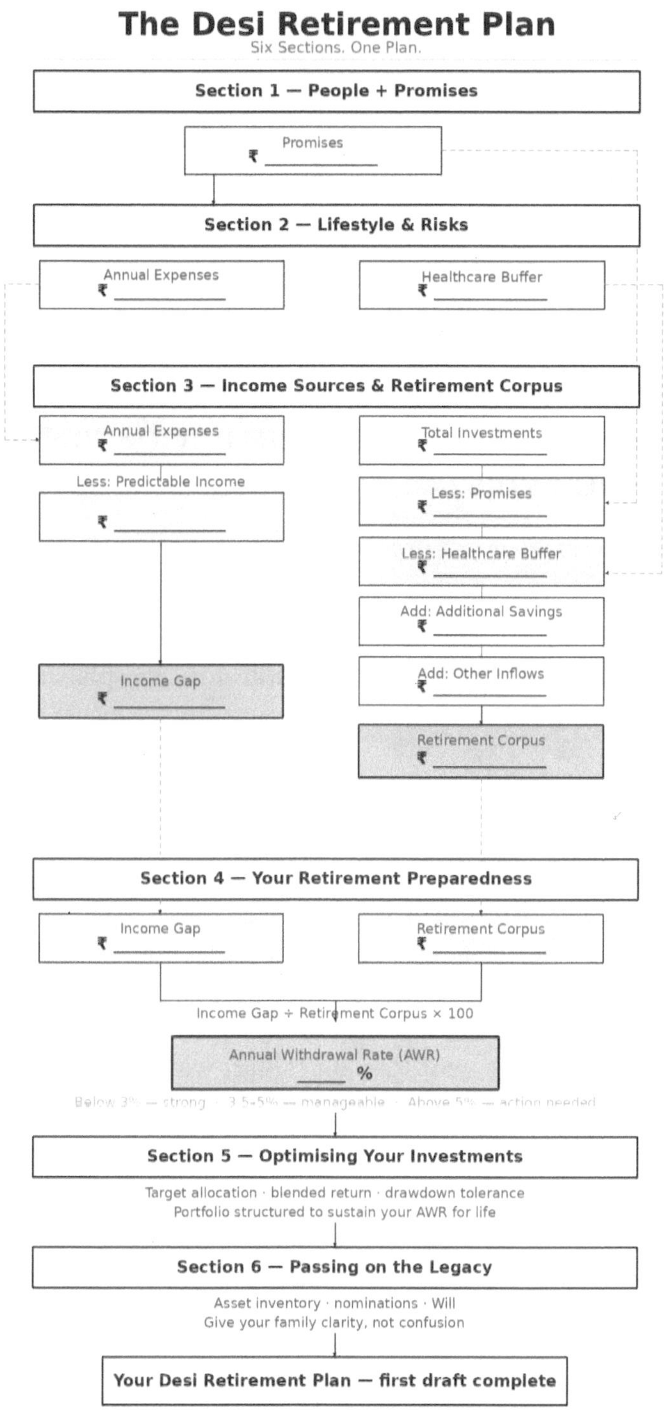
The Desi Retirement Plan
Six Sections. One Plan.
Section 1 — People + Promises
Promises
₹
Section 2 — Lifestyle & Risks
Annual Expenses
₹
Healthcare Buffer
₹
Section 3 — Income Sources & Retirement Corpus
Annual Expenses
₹
Less: Predictable Income
₹
Income Gap
₹
Total Investments
₹
Less: Promises
₹
Less: Healthcare Buffer
₹
Add: Additional Savings
₹
Add: Other Inflows
₹
Retirement Corpus
₹
Section 4 — Your Retirement Preparedness
Income Gap
₹
Retirement Corpus
₹
Income Gap ÷ Retirement Corpus × 100
Annual Withdrawal Rate (AWR)
%
Below 3% — strong · 3.5-5% — manageable · Above 5% — action needed
Section 5 — Optimising Your Investments
Target allocation · blended return · drawdown tolerance
Portfolio structured to sustain your AWR for life
Section 6 — Passing on the Legacy
Asset inventory · nominations · Will
Give your family clarity, not confusion
Your Desi Retirement Plan — first draft complete

Sections 1 through 4 build on each other. Do not skip them. Section 5 is the most technically demanding of the six, as you need a basic idea of investing to complete it. If some of it feels unfamiliar on the first pass, that is fine. Fill in what you can and come back to it after reading the investment chapters. Section 6 is emotionally harder than technically hard, as it deals with the subject of legacy planning. Many people put it off precisely because it forces a conversation they would rather not have. Do not let that happen.

THIS CHAPTER ASKS YOU TO COMPLETE YOUR FIRST DRAFT OF THE PLAN. NOT YOUR FINAL DRAFT. YOUR FIRST.

The goal at this stage is not precision; it is perspective. You are trying to see all six dimensions of your retirement at once, even roughly, so that you know where you stand and where the gaps are. The chapters that follow will help you sharpen each section until the plan reflects your reality rather than your guesswork.

With that in mind, let us begin.

SECTION 1: PEOPLE & PROMISES

We begin by making a shift that sounds simple but is quite significant. We move from asking "How much do I need?" to asking "Who am I planning for?"

Every Desi Retirement Plan must start with one honest question: Who depends on me financially, now and in the future? This is your core circle.

It may include your spouse, your parents or in-laws, children who are still studying or likely to pursue higher education, the siblings or relatives you support quietly, the ones for whom you are the default safety net. If you leave even one person out at this stage, the plan will look healthy on paper and fail in real life.

For each person in your circle, the next question is: what have you promised them? A child's education abroad. A wedding. A home loan you are still repaying. Regular support for ageing parents. Each of these is a financial commitment with a cost and a timeline.

And then there is one more name to add to the list—yours. This is also the time to recognise your promise to yourself. Your bucket list. If you wish to travel, take up a passion, or simply live well in your retirement years, write it down here and budget for it. It is not an afterthought; it is a legitimate financial goal.

Completing this section is a significant milestone. You will have full clarity on everyone who depends on you, every promise you have made, and your own aspirations. That foundation determines the integrity of everything that follows.

Go to Section 1: People & Promises of your Desi Retirement Plan and fill it in now.

SECTION 2: LIFESTYLE & RISKS

In this section, we estimate what your retirement will cost, and then we look honestly at what could derail it.

Start by visualising your life in retirement. Not your life today. The life you expect to live once you stop working. Then begin estimating expenses at today's costs. Do not worry about the exact figures yet—a reasonable estimate beats a precise number that never gets written down. If you do not want to go through the grind of estimating each element, you can start by assuming an annual expense. You will have plenty of opportunity to refine these later.

We then move on to the risks. These risks can derail the best of retirement plans.

The first risk is medical. Health insurance is necessary, but in my experience, almost every Indian family eventually learns that it is not sufficient. Monthly medicines, diagnostics, doctor visits, caregiving costs, and medical inflation that runs faster than almost everything else, health insurance covers part of this. You pay the rest. In this section, you capture your insurance cover, set aside a dedicated healthcare buffer, and establish an emergency liquidity line so that a medical crisis does not force you to liquidate investments at the wrong time.

The second big risk is inflation. This is compounded even more by the gains we have made in longevity. You are likely to live longer than you think, and inflation will hurt more in the later years of your retirement than it does today. The fatal mistake most people make is underestimating both. In this section, you will project your expenses forward—10, 20, 30 years from now. Do not try to be precise. Your best estimate is all that is needed at this stage.

Go to Section 2: Lifestyle & Risks of your Desi Retirement Plan and fill it in now.

SECTION 3: INCOME SOURCES & RETIREMENT CORPUS

This section answers the question that sits at the heart of every retirement plan: how much money do you have available to fund your retirement?

We begin with predictable income—pension, rental income, or any other source you can reliably count on in retirement. Note that interest and dividends from investments are not included here; those are captured separately through your portfolio. Once you have your predictable income, subtract it from your estimated annual expenses, and you arrive at the **Income Gap**. This is the amount that must be funded by your retirement corpus.

Arriving at the retirement corpus is a step that deserves care. It is not simply the total of all your investments. Your self-owned home and jewellery for personal use, for instance, are not part of this calculation—they are assets, but they are not retirement funding assets. From your total investment corpus, you deduct the funds already committed to your promises from Section 1 and your healthcare buffer from Section 2. To what remains, you add the expected growth of your investments between now and retirement, your future savings through SIPs or other means, and any other inflows you can reasonably anticipate—insurance policy payouts or an inheritance, for example.

This is your retirement corpus: the money that is free, unencumbered, and available to meet your expenses in retirement.

Go to Section 3: Income Sources & Retirement Corpus of your Desi Retirement Plan and fill it in now.

SECTION 4: YOUR RETIREMENT PREPAREDNESS

You have now reached the moment of truth.

Section 4 takes everything from Sections 2 and 3 and distils it into one number—the Annual Withdrawal Rate, or AWR. You calculate it by dividing your income gap in the first year of retirement by your retirement corpus, then expressing the result as a percentage. A single number, and yet it tells you more about the health of your retirement plan than almost anything else.

An AWR below 3% means your corpus is strong relative to your spending—you are in excellent shape. Between 3% and 5%, your plan is manageable but requires discipline and conscious decision-making. Above 5%, the plan needs attention.

If your AWR comes out higher than you hoped, do not be alarmed. This is a first draft. The purpose of this exercise is not to arrive at a perfect number—it is to see clearly where you stand. Many people find that their first AWR is uncomfortable. That discomfort is valuable. It tells you exactly where the work needs to be done.

Once you have your AWR, list the action points that could improve it: trimming discretionary expenses, deferring a large spend by a few years, working a little longer, generating part-time income in retirement, or improving your investment returns. You do not need to solve everything here. You need to name the levers.

Go to Section 4: Your Retirement Preparedness of your Desi Retirement Plan and fill it in now.

SECTION 5: OPTIMISING YOUR INVESTMENT PORTFOLIO FOR RETIREMENT

In three decades of working in the financial industry, I have not met a single person whose investment portfolio was genuinely optimised for retirement. That is not a criticism. It is simply the reality of how portfolios are built—incrementally, reactively, shaped by what worked in the past rather than by what will be needed in the future.

The investments you have accumulated were not made with retirement in mind. They were made with the goal of growing as safely and as fast as possible. And the experiences along the way, the investments that worked, and especially the ones that did not, shaped your thinking. Over time, those experiences became biases. And those biases are now embedded in your portfolio.

This section asks you to do three things. First, identify your biases. Whichever asset class dominates your portfolio or is conspicuously absent from it is a bias. An overconcentration in real estate is a bias. An excess of fixed deposits beyond what is genuinely useful is a bias. An underallocation to equity because equity once hurt you is a bias. Name them.

Second, set realistic long-term return assumptions for each asset class: debt, equities, precious metals, and real estate. Not the returns you hope for—the returns you can genuinely expect over the long term.

Third, understand your drawdown tolerance. A drawdown is the maximum fall in the value of your investments that you can stomach during adverse market conditions, without panicking, without selling, without letting the short-term losses damage your long-term plan. Equities, for example, can drop more than 50% in the worst conditions. These situations are uncommon, but you will encounter them in your retirement years. Your target portfolio should be one whose drawdown you can live with.

If some of this feels unfamiliar, do not let it stop you from completing the section. Fill in what you can. This is a starting point. The book devotes two full parts to investments, and by the time you have worked through those chapters, you will have everything you need to return here and sharpen this section considerably.

Go to Section 5: Optimising Your Investments of your Desi Retirement Plan and fill it in now.

SECTION 6: PASSING ON THE LEGACY

The final section looks beyond you.

Your wealth should support your family and not divide it. One clear plan, made today, prevents years of pain tomorrow. And yet this is the section most people put off, partly because it requires confronting mortality, partly because it seems complicated. It is neither as morbid nor as complicated as it appears.

You begin by building an inventory of everything you own—property, bank accounts, investments, insurance policies. Then you check that nominations are in place and that contact details are up to date across every account. Finally, you address the Will—whether it is prepared, in progress, or not yet started. If it has not yet started, the section asks you to at least name your executor and note your intentions.

You do not need a lawyer to begin. You need a list. Start there.

Go to Section 6: Passing on the Legacy of your Desi Retirement Plan and fill it in now.

WHAT COMES NEXT

You have now completed your first draft of the Desi Retirement Plan.

How do you feel? Exhausted, perhaps. Possibly a little relieved. Maybe unsettled by what some of the numbers are telling you. All of that is appropriate. A first draft done honestly will surface things you would rather not have seen, and that discomfort is not a problem—it is the plan working exactly as it should.

What comes next is refinement. Each of the subsequent chapters in this book is written to help you return to one or more of these six sections with greater knowledge, sharper numbers, and a clearer sense of what the plan needs. Some chapters will confirm what you have already written; others will ask you to revisit it.

You can work through the chapters sequentially, building your understanding step by step. Or you can go directly to the section that is weighing on you most, the one where your numbers felt uncertain, or where you knew you were guessing. Both approaches work. What matters is that you eventually engage seriously with all six dimensions.

You may also notice that certain ideas recur across chapters. This is deliberate. Retirement planning is deeply interconnected—a decision about your investments shapes your income gap, which shapes your AWR, which determines everything else. Returning to the same idea from a different angle is not repetition; it is how understanding deepens.

Your retirement plan is not a one-time exercise. It evolves. It sharpens. It demands reflection.

In the end, what you need is a plan that reflects your realities. Not your hopes, not your anxieties—your realities. Keep returning to it. Keep refining it. And trust that the work you have done here—imperfect, incomplete, but honest is the only foundation worth building on.

THE DESI RETIREMENT PLAN

Six Sections. One Plan.

Your name: ______________ Last Updated: ______________

Your Age: ___ Retirement Age: ___ Years to Retirement: ____

SECTION 1: PEOPLE & PROMISES

WHO DEPENDS ON YOU, AND WHAT HAVE YOU PROMISED THEM?

Pro Tip: Do not edit this list for comfort. Write down, every person, every promise, every expectation—spoken or unspoken. It is also important to write down your promise to yourself—your bucket list! If someone or some promise is missing here, the plan will fail in real life even if it looks perfect on paper.

MY CORE CIRCLE AND OBLIGATIONS

Name	Relationship	Promise	Amount (₹)	When? (xx yrs.)

REFLECTION & NOTES:

Who in my life depends on me in ways I may not have acknowledged?

____

____

____

SECTION 2: LIFESTYLE & RISKS

What will your retirement life cost? What could derail it?

Pro Tip: Begin by visualising your lifestyle in retirement. Then estimate your expenses. Break expenses into essential and desirable. For a detailed analysis, a complete list of expenses is provided in Annexure I: Expense Heads. You can adjust the quarterly spends to monthly or annual expenses. Also, budget for expenses that occur once every few years (e.g., vehicle replacement).

RETIREMENT EXPENSES (YOUR FUTURE LIFE AT TODAY'S COSTS)

Monthly Living (Essential)	
	₹
Personal Consumption	
Utilities / Rent	
House Help / Driver	
Local Travel	
Others	
Total Monthly (A)	

Monthly Lifestyle (Desirable)	
	₹
Personal Lifestyle	
Entertainment	
Fitness / Hobbies	
Others	
Total Monthly (B)	

Annual Commitments ₹	
Insurance Premiums	
Education / Fees	
Vacation	
Taxes / Subscriptions	
Medical	
Family Support	
Gifts / Festivals	
Others	
Total Annual (C)	

Periodic Capital Expenses* ₹	
Home Renovation	
Replacement of Gadgets	
Replacement of Vehicle	
Others	
Total Annual (D)	

** Periodic Capital Expenses should be expressed as an annual equivalent (e.g., a ₹5,00,000 vehicle replaced every 10 years = ₹50,000 per year)*

FINAL CALCULATION

Monthly Total (A + B): ________________

Annual from Monthly (×12): ________________

Annual Totals (C + D): ________________

Expense Buffer (10%): ________________

Total Annual Lifestyle Cost: ________________

REFLECTION AND NOTES:

Have I missed any expenses?

____

____

____

MEDICAL RISK

Pro Tip: Health insurance coverage alone is not enough. You need to support it with a Healthcare Buffer and Emergency Liquidity to ensure you can access necessary medical services when needed.

Health Insurance Cover:

Self: ₹_______ Spouse: ₹_______

Family Floater: ₹________

Healthcare Buffer ₹________

Emergency Liquidity Available ₹________

REFLECTION & NOTES:

If a medical emergency occurs, am I financially prepared?

____

____

____

INFLATION PROJECTIONS

Pro Tip: Use your judgement and see how well it aligns with the real numbers later. Annexure-II provides factors you can use to obtain a more accurate estimate of inflation's impact on your expenses.

Description	Value
Annual Expense (Today's Cost) (₹)	
Expected Inflation Rate (%)	
Expense After 10 Years (₹)	
Expense After 20 Years (₹)	
Expense After 30 Years (₹)	
Expense After 40 Years (₹)	

REFLECTION & NOTES:

How realistically have you estimated the inflation rate? What would you do if the inflation rate turned out to be higher than what you had budgeted?

____

____

____

SECTION 3: INCOME SOURCES & RETIREMENT CORPUS

Pro Tip: The purpose of this section is to arrive at the expenses that need to be funded by the retirement corpus. Some part of the expenses will be met by predictable income. The rest needs to be funded by the returns generated from your retirement corpus. In case you do not have any predictable income, just mention "Nil" in this section.

PREDICTABLE INCOME & INCOME GAP

Pension/Annuity (₹): ____________________

Rental Income (₹): ____________________

Others (₹): ____________________

Total Predictable Income (₹) (A) ____________________

Annual Expense (₹) (B): ____________________ (Section 2)

Income Gap (₹) (B-A): ____________________

The income gap is what you need to fund from your retirement corpus.

B. ARRIVING AT YOUR RETIREMENT CORPUS

Pro Tip:

Investment Corpus refers to the total investments that you own today. You have estimated this amount in Chapter 3. First, we set aside funds for promises and the Medical Buffer of the Desi Retirement Plan. Your investments will grow over time—add likely growth in investments. Start with estimates. Refine it with the factors given in Annexure-II. Next, we add estimated savings until retirement (if you are still working) and any other funds (such as payouts from insurance policies or inheritance).

Description	Value
Total Investment Corpus (₹)	
Less: Promises (₹)	
Less: Medical Buffer (₹)	
Add: Investment Growth (₹)	
Add: Future SIP / Savings (₹)	
Add: Funds from Other Sources (₹)	
Total Retirement Corpus (₹)	

REFLECTION & NOTES:

This is the moment of truth. Being aware of where exactly you stand is half the battle won. If this number is too low, you will find ways to improve it in this book.

____

____

____

SECTION 4: YOUR RETIREMENT PREPAREDNESS

Are you truly ready? And if not, what will you do about it?

Pro Tip: The Annual Withdrawal rate (AWR%) can predict if your money will last your lifetime. An AWR below 3% is strong. 3.5% to 5% is manageable with discipline, and above 5% requires a plan of action.

CALCULATING AWR

Annual Expenses (First Year of Retirement) (A): ₹__________ (Section 2)

Retirement Corpus (B): ₹________________

Annual Withdrawal Rate - AWR% ((A/B) *100): ______

Reflection:

Does this number give you confidence or signal a need for action?

____

____

____

IMPROVING YOUR RETIREMENT PREPAREDNESS

Action 1: ____

Action 2: ____

Action 3: ____

Action 4: ____

SECTION 5: OPTIMISING YOUR INVESTMENTS FOR RETIREMENT

Identify your biases. Make realistic assumptions. Correct your portfolio.

Pro Tip:

Your investment experience leads to biases. The biases are reflected in your portfolio (e.g., overconcentration in real estate, excess FD beyond utility, under or overallocation to equity). Make realistic assumptions about long-term returns and expected drawdowns (likely drops in asset value from their peaks in adverse market conditions).

ASSUMPTIONS ON RETURNS / DRAWDOWNS:

Asset Class	Expected Long-Term Returns (% p.a.)	Worst Case Drawdown (%)
Equities		
Debt		
Precious Metals		
Real Estate		

**Drawdown measures the maximum fall in value from peak in % terms. For example, equities can drop over 50% in worst market conditions.*

ASSET ALLOCATION – CURRENT & TARGET

Asset Class	Current Allocation (Amount ₹)	Current Allocation (%)	Target Allocation (%)
Equities			
Debt			
Precious Metals			
Real Estate			
Total		**100%**	**100%**

Metric	Example (Equal 25% each)	Current Allocation (%)	Target Allocation (%)
Blended ROI (% p.a.)	7.75%		
Blended Drawdown (%)	-28.75%		

**Example assumes equal 25% allocation across Equities (10% ROI, 50% drawdown), Debt (6% ROI, 15% drawdown), Gold (7% ROI, 20% drawdown) and Real Estate (8% ROI, 30% drawdown). Blended ROI = (25%×10%) + (25%×6%) + (25%×7%) + (25%×8%) = 7.75%. Blended Drawdown = −(25%×50%) − (25%×15%) − (25%×20%) − (25%×30%) = −28.75%. These numbers are for illustrative purposes only.*

REFLECTION & NOTES:

What biases do I carry about investments? Are the return assumptions consistent with market realities?

____

____

____

SECTION 6: PASSING ON THE LEGACY

Protect what you built. Give your family clarity, not confusion.

Pro Tip: One clear estate plan today prevents years of family pain tomorrow. Build an inventory of all assets. Prioritise the big ones. Get nominations in order. Prepare a Will.

ASSET INVENTORY

S. No.	Asset / Account	Estimated Value (₹)	Nominee Update Yes/No	Contact Details updated (Yes/No)
1.				
2.				
3.				
4.				
5.				
6.				
7.				
8.				
9.				
10.				

WILL & SUCCESSION

	Notes
Will Prepared Yes / No / In progress	
Name of Executor	
Location of Will. Who can access?	
Any special instruction or wishes	

REFLECTION & NOTES:

____

____

____

5

Financial Commitments: The True Cost

This chapter helps you strengthen Section 1 of the Desi Retirement Plan. We began building the plan by identifying the people who depend on us and the promises we have made to them. Now comes the harder question: are the provisions you have made for those promises realistic, or are they dangerously optimistic?

In my experience, the large promises fall into four categories: education and wedding expenses for children, major medical expenses for family members, outstanding loans (typically home loans), and expenses on your own bucket list. These are not monthly costs that blend quietly into your budget. They are lumpy, large, and unavoidable. They arrive at specific points in time and can either be managed with planning or destroy your retirement with panic. Let us make sure you have planned for them properly.

THE EDUCATION QUESTION: WHAT WILL IT ACTUALLY COST?

Ajay's daughter, Priya, was 24 and working at a Bangalore startup when she told him about her MBA plans. She had admits from two schools—IIM Ahmedabad in India, and a solid though not top-tier school in the United States. IIM-A would cost ₹25 lakhs total over two years. The US school would cost ₹50 lakhs, excluding living and travel. Ajay had a total corpus of ₹1.8 crore. Funding the US option meant 28% of his retirement corpus would disappear immediately. IIM-A was 14%. Neither number was comfortable. But at least he knew the number, which meant he could make a real decision rather than an emotional one.

Vague estimates like "education is expensive" are not useful. What is useful is knowing the actual cost range so you can check what you have budgeted against what things cost. **The table below gives current tuition costs, excluding living and travel expenses**, which you will need to add separately.

Education Category	Approx. Cost (₹ in Lakhs)
Tier-1 private engineering — BITS, Manipal, VIT	18 – 30
Mid-tier private undergraduate — India	8 – 12
Government college undergraduate — India	2 – 4
MBA — IIMs (top-tier)	20 – 33
MBA — Tier-2 B-schools	12 – 18
Private medical college — India	50 – 80
Government medical college — India	5 – 10
Undergraduate — US state university	60 – 80
Undergraduate — US private university	150 – 250

**All costs are approximate total programme costs in Indian Rupees (today's value) including tuition, hostel and living expenses. US university costs converted at ₹84/USD.*

For now, use these numbers as a starting point and revalidate them by checking the college's website for the costs.

THE WEDDING QUESTION: BETWEEN TRADITION AND FINANCIAL SUICIDE

Wedding expenses are where desi retirement plans go to die. A disciplined saver, a careful planner, someone who has done everything right, and then a daughter's or son's wedding arrives. Suddenly, ₹40 lakhs, ₹50 lakhs, and even ₹70 lakhs disappear in six months. It is a once-in-a-lifetime event. You do not want to disappoint your family. You want people to remember it. All of this is emotionally true. All of it is financially devastating if it has not been properly planned for.

Let me be direct. I am not advocating for cheap weddings. I am advocating for honest budgeting and conscious choices—not the financial paralysis that comes from social pressure and emotional momentum carrying you past decisions you never actually made. The table below shows what weddings genuinely cost today across three broad tiers.

Category	Budget (₹ in Lakhs)	Mid-Range (₹ in Lakhs)	High-End (₹ in Lakhs)
Venue & Catering	5 – 8	15 – 20	50 – 100
Jewellery (fresh)	8 – 12	12 – 18	20 – 40
Clothes, gifts, misc.	2 – 3	5 – 8	10 – 15
Total	**15 – 23**	**32 – 46**	**60 – 100+**

** Gold prices assumed at ₹7,500 per gram. In certain communities, jewellery requirements may be significantly higher than the ranges shown above.*

THE JEWELLERY REALITY

Jewellery deserves its own paragraph because this is where expectations and reality collide most painfully. A traditional wedding might require a gold necklace, bangles, earrings, and other pieces, which together can run ₹10 to 17 lakhs at current gold prices. If you have been buying gold systematically over the years, small pieces on birthdays and festivals, you may already have ₹8 to 10 lakhs worth accumulated and need to spend only ₹5 to 7 lakhs fresh. But if your child is getting married in a year and you have nothing set aside, you are going to write a ₹15 lakh cheque for jewellery alone. There is no gentle way around that number.

If your child is 15 years old and likely to marry in 10 years, start buying one small piece of gold every year. By the time the wedding arrives, you have accumulated 10 pieces, and the cost has been spread over a decade. This is one of the most practical retirement planning moves available to a desi household.

The second-largest variables after jewellery are the guest count and the venue. A 200-person wedding at a modest hall is financially manageable for most families. An 800-person wedding at a five-star hotel is not unless you are genuinely wealthy enough that this does not meaningfully reduce your retirement corpus. Be honest about which category you are in before the bookings are made, not after.

THE HOME LOAN QUESTION

If you are to enter retirement with an outstanding home loan, you need to address this explicitly rather than letting it drift. There are two options, and neither is inherently better than the other; the right choice depends on your interest rate, tax situation, liquidity needs, and how comfortable you are carrying debt into retirement.

The first option is to pay off the loan at retirement using your corpus. This reduces your corpus immediately but also eliminates the monthly EMI from your expenses going forward. If you have ₹2 crores in corpus and a ₹30 lakh loan outstanding, you start retirement with ₹1.7 crores and ₹25,000 less in monthly outgoings. The second option is to keep paying the EMI from your retirement income, treating it as a known monthly expense for however many years remain on the loan. Either approach can work, but you must choose one, calculate the numbers, and budget accordingly.

If you have five years until retirement and eight years left on your loan, the question to answer now is: will you aggressively prepay to finish it before you retire, or will you budget for three more years of EMI after retirement? Decide, calculate, and write the number down. A decision deferred is not a decision made.

PROMISES TO SELF: THE DREAMS YOU HAVE DEFERRED LONG ENOUGH

There is a category of retirement expenses that most people either skip entirely or feel guilty about including. I call it obligations to self—the bucket list items postponed for decades while meeting every other obligation to everyone else. The trip to Europe you have been talking about since your honeymoon 35 years ago. The photography course you never had time for. Six months in a hill station doing nothing but reading and walking. Learning classical music seriously. Taking your grandchildren on a trip they will remember for the rest of their lives.

These are not luxuries. These are the reasons you worked for 40 years. And I want to be very direct about something that most financial planning books do not say clearly enough: if you do not spend money on your dreams in your sixties and early seventies, when you are healthy enough to enjoy them, you will spend it on hospital bills in your eighties when you are too sick to enjoy anything. The money will be spent either way. The only question is whether you spend it on life or on survival.

When I ask retirees what they regret most, nobody ever says "I wish I had saved more money." They say, "I wish I had taken that trip." "I wish I had learned to paint when I still had steady hands." "I wish I had thrown that big family party when everyone was still around."

This is why I insist you earmark money specifically for obligations to self when building your Desi Retirement Plan. Not as something to think about if money is left, but as a dedicated, non-negotiable allocation, the same as your children's wedding fund or your healthcare buffer.

The truth about bucket lists is that they have expiration dates. The trek to Everest base camp needs to happen before your knees give out. International travel needs to happen before long flights become unbearable. The family reunion needs to happen while your siblings are still alive and mobile. These dreams do not wait patiently for the right moment. They disappear one by one as health declines, energy fades, people pass away, and opportunities close.

The number may feel large—₹10 lakhs, ₹15 lakhs, even ₹20 lakhs. You may feel hesitant to put that much towards things that feel non-essential when you are worried about the sustainability of your retirement. But consider this: the person who retires with ₹3 crores and spends ₹15 lakhs on dreams in the first decade, then lives contentedly on ₹2.85 crores, has planned better than the person who retires with ₹3 crores, spends nothing on themselves, lives with regret and depression, and dies at 78, leaving ₹3.5 crores to children who would have preferred a happier parent.

Your children do not need your money as much as they need your happiness. Your corpus does not need to grow forever. It needs to support a life worth living. Write your bucket list honestly, cost it realistically, set aside the money specifically, and then this is the part that requires the most discipline—actually spend it. In the first five to 10 years of retirement, while you are healthy, while the dreams are still possible, while the people you want to share them with are still around. Do not let fear of the future rob you of joy in the present.

Everything covered in this chapter—education costs, wedding provisions, outstanding loans, and bucket list allocations represents money that needs to be set aside from your corpus and earmarked for specific purposes. It is not available for generating retirement income. It exists to honour the commitments you have already made, to others and to yourself.

Go back to Section 1 of your Desi Retirement Plan. Check every number against the ranges in this chapter. Ask whether each provision is realistic or wishful. Adjust the figures until you are confident; they reflect the actual cost of the actual promise. In the next chapter, we turn to your retirement expenses, and after that, we will apply inflation to everything.

6

Estimating Retirement Expenses Accurately

Chapters 6 to 9 help you strengthen Section 2 - Lifestyle & Risks of the Desi Retirement Plan.

Retirement planning is not a question about money. It is a question about lifestyle. And the answers are as diverse as people themselves. Some dream of moving back to their hometown, closer to familiar streets, old friends, and extended family. Others choose to stay in the city where they've spent most of their working life, surrounded by the comfort of established routines and modern conveniences. A few even imagine starting afresh—buying a new place, moving to a quieter suburb, or relocating near the sea or mountains.

Take Mr. Sharma, for example. After retiring from a corporate job in Mumbai, he decided to move back to Lucknow, where his roots were. Life there is slower, costs are lower, and he is surrounded by cousins and childhood friends. For him, retirement was about *belonging*. His expenses dropped significantly, but his quality of life improved because he chose a lifestyle that matched his personality.

On the other hand, Mrs. Iyer, a retired teacher in Bengaluru, chose to stay right where she was. Her children and grandchildren live in the city, and she enjoys the buzz of urban life. She spends more on rent and utilities than she would in her native town, but for her, the joy of being close to family and having access to good healthcare outweighs the extra cost. For her, retirement was about *connection.*

These choices—where to live, whether to own or rent, whether to downsize or upgrade—are not small decisions. They are the bedrock of retirement planning. Each path leads to a very different set of expenses, and those expenses will shape your financial needs for decades.

This is why retirement planning is not just about numbers on a spreadsheet; it's about real-life choices. It's about asking, "What do I value most?" *Comfort? Freedom? Family? Security? Adventure?* Once you answer these questions honestly, the numbers will follow naturally.

Think of it this way: before you can decide how much petrol your car needs, you must decide where you are driving. Retirement is exactly like that. Define the destination first—the life you want. Only then can you estimate your expenses accurately. Finally, you can determine the fuel—your retirement corpus and income—that is needed to meet your lifestyle expenses.

Most retirement guides treat your golden years as a flat, unchanging expense line. But here's the truth they won't tell you: retirement isn't one long, steady phase. It's three distinct acts in your life's greatest performance. A deeper understanding of these phases will help you plan your expenses more realistically.

THE THREE ACTS OF YOUR RETIREMENT STORY

ACT I: THE ADVENTURE YEARS (YEARS 1–5)

You've waited decades to climb Machu Picchu, to take that Mediterranean cruise, to learn pottery in Tuscany. This is your bucket list season, where expenses can soar as you finally have time to do the things that you always wanted to but never had the time to do so.

Act II: The Active Years (Years 6–20)

Your pace settles into a sustainable rhythm. You're healthy, engaged, balancing core needs with discretionary pleasures—regular dining out, annual vacations, hobbies, and social activities.

ACT III: THE COMFORT YEARS (YEARS 21+)

Life simplifies. Core expenses dominate, healthcare needs may increase, but without major ailments, the pending naturally contracts to essentials and simple pleasures.

Understanding these phases changes everything about how you plan. It helps you transform your retirement from a financial guessing game into a masterfully orchestrated life.

There are two important dimensions on which you will have to think about expenses to estimate them accurately.

First, your expenses are not evenly spread over the year.

Second, you need to be able to make a clear distinction between essential and desirable expenses. This is important because your income is variable, especially if your primary source of funding is investment income. In extreme situations, it would be prudent to cut your desirable expenses.

Let us examine each of the dimensions in greater detail.

The first dimension relates to your annual spending pattern. Many expenses are incurred monthly. Rent, utility bills, groceries, local travel, domestic help, medicines, etc.

However, there are equally many other expenses that you would incur during the year that are either quarterly, semi-annually, or annually. These expenses could relate to insurance premiums, vacations, gadgets, personal accessories, birthday and anniversary celebrations, etc.

If you only budget for the monthly items, you'll be caught off guard when the bigger ones come due. The secret is to anticipate irregular expenses and spread their cost across years.

Hence, the starting point is to build an expense estimate that captures all expenses, regardless of timing.

ESSENTIAL VS DESIRABLE EXPENSES

All your expenses can be categorised in these two buckets—Essential or Desirable. As the name suggests, essential expenses are those that you cannot do away with under any circumstances.

Essential expenses are the "MUST HAVE" expenses. In today's day and age, it is not just "Roti, Kapada, and Makaan"; you must stay connected to the world and invest in internet connectivity. Also, a basic holiday can be counted as a core expense.

These expenses include:

Household groceries and utilities

Housing costs (rent, maintenance, property taxes, or society charges)

Basic clothing and personal care

Medical insurance premiums

Out-of-pocket healthcare costs, annual health checkups, healthy-living expenses, gym membership, trainer cost

Transportation and commuting

Loan EMIs (if any remain)

Taxes

On the other hand, some expenses are desirable in nature.

Desirable expenses are "NICE TO HAVE" expenses. An international holiday or spending on the most expensive smartphone could fall into this category.

I do not want to get into any value judgement here. What could be desirable for someone could be an essential expense for someone else. The only reason we are doing this segregation up front is so that, if a situation demands a cut in expenses, you know what to cut and where to focus.

These are lifestyle choices. They add comfort, joy, and fulfilment, but can be adjusted if finances are tight.

Examples include:

Vacations and travel

Dining out

Gifting (festivals, weddings, grandchildren's birthdays)

Hobbies, memberships, and leisure activities

Upgrading gadgets, furniture, or appliances

Philanthropy or religious donations

These are not compulsory, but they are equally important for a happy retirement. After all, retirement isn't just about survival—it's about living well.

Now that you have a fair idea of how to think about your retirement expenses, it is time to estimate them.

In **Annexure-I: Expense Heads,** I have provided a comprehensive list of all the expense categories. All you need to do is go through the list and estimate the expenses that you are likely to incur in each of these categories.

You would also notice that you can input these expenses either as Essential or Desirable, the second dimension on which you need to think about your expenses.

When you fill in the details, think about your Active Years—this is the period when you have a kind of steady rhythm to your retired life.

PRO TIP:

Do not rush to complete this exercise. First, think through the lifestyle that you would like to lead in your retirement years. Next, estimate the expenses.

You would agree that if your expense estimate is inaccurate, the complete retirement plan would be worthless, as the core idea of the plan is to meet your expenses.

In the next chapter, I want to discuss a very important aspect of managing expenses—the emotional traps that make you overspend, and many retirees end up regretting it later.

7

How Can Emotions Derail Your Retirement?

Retirement planning isn't about numbers and charts; it's about emotions, values, and the people we love. Many financial decisions are made not with calculators, but with the heart. We stretch to give our children "the best," help relatives in crisis, or hold on to a lifestyle that makes us feel accomplished. These choices often come from a good place, but if unchecked, they can quietly erode the foundation of our own financial security. The goal is not to love less, but to spend with awareness and balance.

THE LOVE TRAP - OVERSPENDING ON CHILDREN

One of the most common emotional pitfalls is going beyond our means for our children's education or weddings. Parents often equate financial sacrifice with love, imagining that a college degree from an expensive university or a lavish wedding guarantees future happiness. Giving too much too soon can deprive both generations—the parents of a secure retirement, and the children of financial discipline. Love also includes teaching independence and responsibility. Instead of exhausting one's retirement savings, consider sharing costs, setting clear limits, or helping children earn scholarships and manage their own finances.

I'm not saying don't spend on education and weddings. I'm saying decide how much you can spend without jeopardising your future, then spend within that limit—even if relatives' gossip, even if it's "less than" your neighbour's wedding, even if your child is initially disappointed.

Because, you know, what's more disappointing is having to move in with your children at age 72 because you ran out of money and becoming the financial burden you swore you'd never become.

THE PRIDE DILEMMA - MAINTAINING APPEARANCES

Another emotional trap is lifestyle inflation—the quiet pressure to "keep up" with friends or colleagues even after regular income stops. The pride of having "made it" can lead retirees to maintain cars, homes, or memberships that no longer serve their real happiness. Pride is costly when it outlives purpose. Simplifying life is not a step down; it's a step towards freedom. True dignity in retirement comes not from appearances, but from peace of mind and choice.

THE GUILT RESPONSE - HELPING GROWN CHILDREN AGAIN AND AGAIN

Parents often step in to rescue adult children from financial troubles—loans, business losses, or credit card debt out of guilt or protectiveness. But repeated financial bailouts can delay or destroy one's own stability. Offering advice, connecting them to financial planners, or helping them set realistic budgets are better forms of support. Emotional generosity doesn't mean financial recklessness. Remember: if you fall short later, those same children may carry the burden of supporting you, creating a new emotional strain for everyone.

THE FAMILY PRESSURE - OBLIGATIONS TO EXTENDED RELATIVES

In our culture, supporting siblings, ageing parents, or relatives in need is seen as both a duty and a virtue. While compassion is essential, unplanned financial help can quickly become unsustainable. It helps to set clear boundaries—decide what you can give regularly without jeopardising your own plans. Create a "giving fund" as part of your annual budget so generosity has a structure. This allows you to help without guilt and keeps your long-term goals on track.

BALANCING EMOTION AND LOGIC

Being financially wise doesn't mean being cold-hearted. In fact, the most successful retirees are those who blend reason with compassion—caring for others while ensuring they remain independent. One approach is to look at retirement savings as a safety net, not just for you but for your family's stability later. When your needs are secure, you can give more meaningfully, without fear or resentment. Financial freedom isn't selfish; it's a gift that keeps on giving because a secure retiree can support others out of choice, not necessity.

PRACTICAL WAYS TO BALANCE HEART AND HEAD

Set written boundaries for major spending—education, weddings, or support to relatives. A budget in writing tempers emotions in the moment.

Keep an emergency reserve strictly for personal and medical use, untouchable for any other reason.

Involve your spouse and children in conversations about retirement goals so expectations are clear.

Build emotional resilience—learn to say, "I wish I could, but I can't right now." This sentence can save your future.

Review your finances annually to spot emotional overspending early and correct course with professional guidance.

THE REWARD - PEACE AND DIGNITY IN LATER YEARS

Retirement should not feel like a punishment for loving too much. It can be a joyful, purposeful phase—if emotions are guided by clarity. When you protect your financial independence, you're also protecting your self-respect and your family's peace of mind. The best gift you can give to your loved ones is not money today, but the example of a life lived responsibly, with warmth and wisdom. Emotional spending fades; emotional intelligence endures.

In the next chapter, we will focus on the biggest unknown in retirement—funding medical emergencies.

8

Funding Medical Emergencies

Dr. Sharma—yes, he is a doctor himself—retired at 62 from a long career as a cardiologist in Delhi. He had spent decades watching patients struggle with medical bills, and he was determined not to be one of them. He had accumulated ₹2.5 crores through careful saving and wise investing. He had comprehensive health insurance with ₹25 lakh coverage. He felt bulletproof. His monthly expenses when he retired were ₹80,000, of which about ₹12,000 was medical, routine checkups, a few maintenance medications for cholesterol and blood pressure, and the occasional diagnostic test. Nothing serious.

Then came the phone call at 3 AM.

His wife had collapsed in the bathroom. Chest pain, difficulty breathing, and cold sweats. He knew the signs immediately. The ambulance arrived within 20 minutes. Emergency angiography at the hospital showed three major blockages. She needed immediate bypass surgery. The hospital was not on his insurance network's cashless list, but there was no time to transfer her—her condition was critical. Dr. Sharma signed the consent forms. The surgery was successful. His wife survived. But when he went to settle the hospital bill five days later, the number on the invoice made his hands shake: ₹18.5 lakhs.

He had insurance, ₹25 lakhs of coverage. But here is what he discovered at the hospital billing counter. The insurance company required forms to be filled out, documents to be submitted, and a waiting period of 15 to 21 days for non-network hospitals. It was reimbursement, not cashless. Several expenses were not covered: the premium room his wife needed for post-surgery monitoring exceeded the policy's room-rent cap, certain medicines and consumables were not on the approved list, and the surgeon's fees exceeded the policy's standard rate. After all the paperwork, claims, and partial rejections, his insurance covered ₹11 lakhs. He had to pay ₹7.5 lakhs out of pocket. Immediately.

"I am a doctor. I spent my whole career treating cardiac patients. I had insurance. I thought I was prepared. But when it actually happened, I realised insurance was just the first line of defence, and it was not enough."

This is the healthcare reality that most retirement plans completely miss. Insurance does not solve the healthcare cost problem. It merely reduces it. And in a medical emergency, you need real, accessible money right now—not after the insurance company processes your claim in three weeks.

THE HEALTHCARE INFLATION TIME BOMB

Dr. Sharma's story is the crisis. What follows is the slow burn. Ramesh Uncle, as his neighbourhood calls him, is 71 years old and lives in Pune. He is generally healthy, other than mild diabetes, blood pressure medication, and the occasional joint pain. In 2019, his monthly medical expenses came to about ₹8,000. Today, those same expenses are ₹22,000 per month. The medicines are the same. The doctors are the same. The tests are the same. But the prices have nearly tripled in five years. His diabetes medication went from ₹450 to ₹950; his blood pressure pills from ₹280 to ₹620; his quarterly blood tests from ₹1,200 to ₹2,800; and his doctor's consultation fee from ₹800 to ₹1,600.

What followed over the next decade was not a single catastrophe but an inexorable escalation. At 74, a minor heart scare required angioplasty, insurance covered the surgery, but follow-up medications and monthly cardiology consultations pushed monthly medical spending to ₹38,000. At 78, his wife developed arthritis requiring expensive medication and physiotherapy, bringing their combined medical expenses to ₹65,000. At 82, Ramesh Uncle himself needed a knee replacement; insurance covered the surgery, but a full-time attendant for three months, physiotherapy for six months, and ongoing pain management pushed monthly medical costs to ₹85,000. By age 84, their total monthly expenses were ₹2.1 lakhs, of which ₹95,000 was medical. His original retirement budget of ₹80,000 a month had more than doubled, not because they were living lavishly, but because healthcare costs had exploded.

His corpus, which had grown to ₹2.8 crores by age 70, was now down to ₹90 lakhs. At current spending rates, he had perhaps four to five years of money left. He was 84 years old. His wife was 82. Both were likely to live into their early nineties.

"I spent my whole career treating patients. I understood healthcare costs better than most people. And even I underestimated what would happen to my own medical expenses in old age."

This is the healthcare time bomb sitting ticking in almost every retirement plan. You plan for 5%–6% inflation. You might budget a little extra for medical expenses. But you cannot truly account for the exponential increase in healthcare costs as you move from your sixties into your seventies and then your eighties. The progression is not linear. It accelerates.

Before discussing the three-layer defence strategy, two practical points are worth making. First, the government has established Jana Aushadhi Kendras across the country, which dispense genuine generic medicines at significantly lower prices than branded equivalents. Ask your doctor for the generic name of every medication you are prescribed, and you can often obtain the same drug at a fraction of the cost. Second, several diagnostic chains now offer bundled health check-up packages at competitive rates. The annual tests you need for routine monitoring of chronic conditions can often be done at a third of the cost of unbundled tests at premium centres. These two habits alone can meaningfully reduce your monthly medical spend.

The Three-Layer Healthcare Defence

After watching hundreds of retirees struggle with healthcare costs, some bankrupted by a single emergency, others slowly drained by rising chronic care expenses, the solution is not a single instrument but a system of three concentric layers of protection, each catching what the previous layer missed.

Layer 1 is your health insurance.

Layer 2 is your healthcare buffer.

Layer 3 is your emergency credit line.

You need all three. Insurance alone leaves you vulnerable to the gaps. Savings alone leave you exposed to catastrophic costs. Having neither means one serious illness can wipe out your entire retirement plan.

LAYER 1: HEALTH INSURANCE - YOUR FIRST LINE OF DEFENCE

There is no substitute for health insurance. None. Without it, a single major illness can destroy decades of saving, regardless of how large your corpus is. But having insurance and having the right insurance are two vastly different things. Most people buy health insurance the way they buy car insurance. They focus on the premium and the coverage amount, sign the papers, and forget about it until they need it. Then, standing at the hospital billing counter in the middle of a medical crisis, they discover all the gaps.

HOW MUCH COVER IS ENOUGH

Twenty years ago, ₹5 lakh coverage seemed adequate. Ten years ago, ₹10 lakhs felt comfortable. Today, if you are retiring with anything less than ₹20–25 lakhs of coverage per person, you are underinsured. Cardiac bypass surgery at a decent hospital in Mumbai or Delhi easily costs ₹12–18 lakhs. A hip replacement costs ₹8 to 12 lakhs. Cancer treatment can consume ₹20–40 lakhs over a year. A week-long ICU stay for any serious condition—pneumonia, kidney failure, stroke can hit ₹5 to 7 lakhs. And healthcare inflation is running at 12%–15% annually. That ₹25 lakh cover today will feel like a ₹10 lakh cover in seven years. Aim for ₹25–30 lakhs per person as the minimum, and consider a family floater for you and your spouse rather than separate individual policies; it is more economical and gives you flexibility in how cover is used.

THE WAITING PERIODS THAT CATCH PEOPLE OUT

There are three types of waiting periods to understand before you sign anything. The initial waiting period, usually 30 days, means that an illness that develops immediately after you buy a policy will not be covered. Only accidents are typically covered from day one. The pre-existing disease waiting period is the one that truly catches people. Most policies impose a two to four-year wait before covering conditions you were already diagnosed with when you bought the policy. Diabetes, hypertension, arthritis, thyroid conditions—all are subject to this wait. It extends further than most people realise: a passing mention of chest pain in your medical records three years ago could allow an insurance company to classify a heart attack as pre-existing. If you are 55 and buying insurance, a four-year pre-existing waiting period means you will not be fully covered until you are 59, precisely when risk is climbing fastest. Seek policies with one to two year maximums or pay the higher premium for immediate pre-existing coverage. Finally, disease-specific waiting periods apply to certain procedures regardless of pre-existing status—joint replacement, hernia, cataracts, and kidney stones often carry their own one to two-year waits. Read every policy's waiting period schedule before you buy.

THE EXCLUSIONS THAT SHOCK PEOPLE

Room-rent capping is the exclusion that surprises most people because it is buried in the fine print. A policy with ₹10 lakh coverage might cap room rent at 1% of the sum insured, meaning ₹10,000 per day for a regular room and ₹20,000 per day for an ICU. If you are actually in an ICU at ₹40,000 per day, you pay ₹20,000 out of pocket every single day. Worse, many policies contain a proportionate deduction clause: if your actual room rent exceeds the cap, the insurer reduces not just the room rent reimbursement but all covered expenses proportionately. Dr. Sharma's wife needed a premium room at ₹35,000 per day. His policy capped rooms at ₹25,000. Because he exceeded the cap, the insurer applied a 30% proportionate deduction to his entire claim—on an ₹18.5 lakh bill, that alone meant ₹5.5 lakhs came out of his pocket. Look for policies with no room-rent capping, or, at a minimum, single-private-room coverage without percentage limits.

Consumables, such as gloves, syringes, bandages, and surgical tape, are excluded by many policies. It sounds minor until you see the bill and realise ₹1 to 2 lakhs of a ₹15 lakh hospitalisation is consumables. Similarly, out-patient expenses—regular doctor visits, blood tests, physiotherapy are typically excluded entirely. For a retiree, these OPD costs are often the larger ongoing expense: Ramesh Uncle's ₹22,000 per month was almost entirely OPD, and his insurance covered none of it. Many policies now offer consumables coverage and OPD riders; they increase the premium meaningfully but are worth considering. Finally, disease-specific sub-limits can cap individual treatments well below the sum insured—cataract surgery at ₹40,000 per eye, joint replacement at ₹2 lakhs, chemotherapy at ₹5 lakhs per year, regardless of the total cover shown on your policy. Read the sub-limit schedule carefully.

CASHLESS VS REIMBURSEMENT: WHY NETWORK MATTERS

Dr. Sharma's nightmare was not only about coverage gaps, but it was also about cash flow. Even if his insurance would eventually cover everything, he still needed ₹18.5 lakhs in hand at the hospital billing counter. Cashless facility means the hospital bills the insurer directly, and you walk out paying only what is genuinely not covered. Reimbursement means you pay the full bill out of pocket, then submit a claim and wait 15 to 45 days for repayment. For a retiree with a fixed corpus, reimbursement can mean liquidating investments at the wrong time, borrowing from family, or taking a personal loan, and if the insurer rejects part of your claim, you absorb that loss permanently. Check how many hospitals in your city are part of your insurer's cashless network, and specifically whether hospitals with strong cardiac, oncology, and orthopaedic units are included. If not, either switch policies or ensure you have sufficient liquid funds on hand at all times.

PRO TIP: Even at a network hospital, cashless is not guaranteed. If a treatment is complex or expensive, the hospital may ask for a deposit up front and settle with insurance later. Always have backup funds accessible. And ensure that someone in your family—your spouse, a child—knows your policy number, the insurer's helpline, and where to find the documents. In a 3 AM emergency, you may not be the one making the calls.

YOUR INSURANCE CHECKLIST

When reviewing your existing policy or evaluating a new one, work through these questions. Is your sum insured at least ₹25–30 lakhs per person? Are pre-existing conditions covered within two years at most? Is there no room-rent cap, or, at a minimum, a single private-room limit without percentage restrictions? Are consumables covered? Is there zero or minimal co-payment? Are all major hospitals in your city in the cashless network? Does the policy offer a restoration benefit that restores the sum insured if it is exhausted mid-year? Does the no-claim bonus increase your cover over time? Is renewability guaranteed for life with no upper age limit? And can you port to this policy from your current one without losing continuity benefits? Finally, do not optimise for the cheapest premium. Health insurance is not the place to save ₹5,000 annually. A better policy will save you lakhs when you need it.

LAYER 2: THE HEALTHCARE BUFFER - YOUR SAFETY NET

Insurance is essential, but it is not enough. You need a dedicated healthcare fund—money set aside specifically for the medical expenses that insurance will not cover or cannot cover quickly enough. Think of this as your health emergency corpus. Just as you had an emergency fund during your working years for unexpected expenses, you need a healthcare fund in retirement for a category of costs that is both predictable in aggregate and deeply unpredictable in timing.

Dr. Sharma had ₹2.5 crores in total corpus but no dedicated healthcare fund. When his wife needed ₹18.5 lakhs immediately, he broke fixed deposits prematurely, sold mutual fund units in a falling market, and borrowed from his children. If he had kept ₹20 lakhs set aside as a healthcare buffer, he could have used it, waited for the insurance company to process the reimbursement, replenished the fund, and incurred no permanent losses. Instead, he crystallised losses that could not be undone.

How Much Should Be in Your Healthcare Buffer

The right amount depends on your age, health status, family history, and the gaps in your insurance coverage. The table below provides a framework.

Your Situation	Recommended Buffer (per person)
Healthy, comprehensive insurance with few gaps	₹3 – 5 lakhs
One or more chronic conditions (diabetes, hypertension, arthritis)	₹8 – 10 lakhs
Family history of cancer, heart disease, or kidney disease	₹10 – 15 lakhs
Insurance with major gaps — high co-pay, restrictive room cap, limited network	₹15 – 20 lakhs

For most retired couples, ₹10 lakhs per person—₹20 lakhs total—is the right starting point. It is not money sitting idle. It is buying something priceless: the ability to get the best treatment at the best hospital without financial panic, without selling investments at the wrong moment, without borrowing from your children.

WHERE TO KEEP THE HEALTHCARE BUFFER

The healthcare buffer has three requirements: it must be liquid—accessible at short notice; it must be safe—not subject to significant volatility; and it must at least keep pace with inflation so it does not silently shrink in real terms over a decade.

A practical approach is to keep roughly half in bank fixed deposits or a conservative debt mutual fund for stability, a portion in a liquid or arbitrage fund for quick access, and a smaller allocation in a hybrid fund for modest inflation protection. Keep this fund in a separate account from your general savings—it should be psychologically and practically ring-fenced. It is touched only for healthcare.

LAYER 3: THE EMERGENCY CREDIT LINE - YOUR LAST RESORT

Even with insurance and a healthcare buffer, there is one more layer you need: an emergency credit line. This is your absolute last resort—the parachute you hope never to use but are grateful to have. Medical emergencies are chaotic. Insurance cashless approval takes time. Your healthcare buffer may be in a fixed deposit that takes two to three days to liquidate. But the hospital wants a deposit now, before treatment begins.

A credit card with a high limit becomes a crucial part of your healthcare strategy, not as a funding source, but as a timing bridge. Consider: it is 2 AM, your spouse has chest pain, and you rush to the hospital. The emergency room doctor wants to admit her immediately. The hospital asks for a ₹50,000 deposit before proceeding. Your insurance company's helpline opens at 9 AM. Your liquid fund redemption will be credited tomorrow afternoon. You swipe your credit card. Treatment begins. Over the next three days, you use the card for a further ₹1 lakh in non-covered expenses. By day four, insurance has approved cashless for covered items. You pay off the card from your healthcare buffer within the interest-free period. No interest. No panic. No permanent loss.

Not any credit card will serve this purpose. You need a high credit limit at minimum ₹5 lakhs, preferably ₹8 to 10 lakhs. Medical bills accumulate quickly, and the limit needs to cover initial deposits, investigations, medicines, and procedures until insurance processes or you can access the healthcare buffer. Know your card's exact interest-free period—typically 30 to 50 days from the transaction date—and pay the full balance within that period. Carrying a balance at 36%–48% annual interest is financially catastrophic for a retiree. The card is a bridge, not a loan.

PRO TIP: Apply for a premium credit card before you retire, while you still have employment income. Banks extend high credit limits far more readily to employed applicants than to retirees living on corpus withdrawals. Once you are two to three years into retirement, getting a ₹8 to 10 lakh limit becomes significantly harder. Act now.

The cardinal discipline: this card is for healthcare emergencies only. Not dining, not traveling, not shopping. When you do use it for a medical emergency, repay it in full within the interest-free period from your healthcare buffer or emergency fund if necessary. The credit card buys you time. It does not provide money you do not have.

THE THREE LAYERS WORKING TOGETHER

Let me show you how this system works in practice. Your spouse has a sudden stroke at 8 PM. You rush to the nearest hospital with a neurology unit.

At 8 PM, the hospital asks for a ₹1 lakh deposit before ICU admission. Your insurer's helpline is closed. You swipe your credit card. Treatment begins immediately.

At 9 AM the next morning, you call the helpline and begin the cashless approval process by submitting the policy number, admission papers, and the doctor's initial assessment. By day two, an insurance officer visits the hospital to verify the case.

By day three, cashless is approved, but the ICU costs ₹15,000 per day, and your policy caps room at ₹8,000, leaving ₹7,000 per day as your responsibility. Consumables and certain medicines are also excluded. On a ₹4.2 lakh bill by day seven, insurance has covered ₹2.8 lakhs, and you have paid ₹1.4 lakhs from your healthcare buffer and credit card.

Your spouse is discharged on day ten. The final bill is ₹5.8 lakhs; insurance covered ₹3.9 lakhs cashless, and your out-of-pocket total is ₹1.9 lakhs.

In week two, you repay the credit card in full from the healthcare buffer within the interest-free period, so no interest is charged.

In week three, you replenish the healthcare buffer by moving money from your debt allocation. The buffer is back to ₹10 lakhs, ready for the next event. Your total out-of-pocket on a ₹5.8 lakh medical crisis: ₹1.9 lakhs, managed calmly and without permanent damage to your corpus.

Without the three-layer system, the same crisis could have meant panic liquidation, permanent investment losses, and borrowing from family.

Layer	Component	What it does
1	Health Insurance (₹25–30 L per person)	Covers major hospitalisation. Reduces catastrophic financial risk. Must have cashless facility at network hospitals.
2	Healthcare Buffer (₹10 L per person)	Covers gaps insurance misses: consumables, room rent excess, OPD, co-payments. Provides funds while waiting for insurance approval.
3	Emergency Credit Card (₹5–10 L limit)	Provides instant liquidity at 2 AM when everything else takes time. Bridges the gap between emergency and insurance approval. Repaid in full within the interest-free period.

Your Healthcare Action Plan

Pull out your actual health insurance policy document—not the marketing brochure, the policy itself with all the fine print. If you do not have it, download it from the insurer's website today. Work through the following: Is your sum insured at least ₹25 lakhs per person? If not, you need to upgrade before the next renewal. What are the waiting periods for pre-existing conditions and specific diseases? If they exceed two years and you are above 55, that is a meaningful gap. Is there a room-rent cap? Calculate what that cap means in rupees in a real ICU scenario—that is, the amount you are personally liable for per day above the cap. Make a list of everything excluded: consumables, OPD, and specific treatments. Estimate the rupee impact of those gaps in a major medical event. And check whether all the major hospitals in your city, specifically those with strong cardiac, oncology, and orthopaedic departments, are in your insurer's cashless network.

Now, calculate your healthcare funding gap. If you had a major medical event costing ₹10 lakhs, how much would your insurance actually cover after all the caps, exclusions, and co-payments? The difference is the minimum you need in your healthcare buffer.

Open a separate account or investment specifically for this fund—do not mix it with your general savings or emergency fund. If you need ₹20 lakhs and currently have nothing allocated, build it over two to three years by moving roughly ₹7 lakhs per year from your corpus into this fund.

Finally, fill in Section 3 of your Desi Retirement Plan: your health insurance sum assured, your healthcare buffer amount ready, and you have enough credit limit on your emergency card. Check that each is adequate. These three numbers and their adequacy are the difference between a healthcare crisis that is managed and one that destroys everything you have built.

HEALTHCARE IS THE WILD CARD

You can estimate lifestyle expenses, model investment returns, and project inflation with reasonable precision. Healthcare is fundamentally different; it is unpredictable in timing, exponential in trajectory, and unforgiving when you are unprepared. You cannot control whether you get sick. You cannot control healthcare inflation. But you can control whether you are financially ready when illness strikes.

Insurance alone is not enough; it has too many gaps. A generic emergency fund is not enough; healthcare needs a dedicated provision. The three-layer system works because it is redundant by design. Each layer backs up the others. Together, they transform healthcare from an existential threat to your retirement into a manageable expense category. They let you focus on getting well instead of panicking about how to pay.

Build your three layers now, while you are healthy and thinking clearly. Do not wait until you are sitting at a hospital billing counter at 3 AM, trying to find ₹15 lakhs by morning.

Your body might write the biggest cheque of your retirement. Make sure you have the funds to cash it.

9

Inflation – The Silent Killer

Before you read further, there are two takeaways from this chapter worth holding in your mind from the start.

First: you need to budget for different inflation rates, with a higher rate specifically for medical expenses. Second: even if you generate a 2%–3% higher investment return than general inflation, there is a meaningful probability that you will run out of money in the later years of retirement. The second one is hard to accept. But when you work through the chapter, the mathematics will make it clear why this happens.

THE PROBLEM NOBODY WANTS TO FACE

Rajiv Malhotra celebrated his 60th birthday in 2024 with a quiet family dinner at his favourite restaurant in Kolkata. His children had flown in from Bangalore and Delhi, his grandchildren sang him a cheerful off-key birthday song, and the atmosphere was warm and full. But even amid the celebration, his mind kept drifting to the future. It seemed so uncertain. He knew he had never truly reflected on what lay ahead, and he wished someone could help him think it through. This is not only Rajiv's reality. It is true for millions of Indians.

India's healthcare has transformed in the past three decades. Diseases that killed our grandparents are now manageable with medication. Heart attacks that would have been fatal in 1990 are survivable with stents and bypass surgeries. The combination of better healthcare, improved nutrition, and advances in medical technology means Indians are living longer than any previous generation. A healthy 60-year-old Indian today has a reasonable probability of living another 30 to 40 years, not a guarantee, but probable enough that planning for it is essential rather than optional.

This should be wonderful news. More time with family, more years to travel, more decades to pursue interests that work never allowed. But there is a silent enemy that turns this blessing into a potential financial catastrophe—so quiet, so gradual, so persistent that most people do not notice it attacking them until the damage is done.

Inflation is like rust on iron. You do not see it happening in real time. But leave the iron exposed long enough, and one day you realise the strength has been eaten away from the inside.

THE INDIAN REALITY

India has been remarkably consistent about one thing over the past two decades: inflation has averaged around 5%–6% per year. Some years higher, some years lower, but over long periods it settles into that range with almost mathematical precision. In 2014, a decent lunch at a local restaurant in Mumbai might have cost ₹150. Today, that same lunch costs ₹250–300. The auto-rickshaw ride that was ₹40 is now ₹70. The electricity bill that was ₹1,800 is now ₹3,200. The household helper who came for ₹3,000 per month now charges ₹6,000. Every price has crept upward.

Most of us adapted during our working years because our incomes were rising too—annual raises, promotions, bonuses. The salary that was ₹5 lakhs in 2014 became ₹10 lakhs by 2024, so we absorbed the price increases without much pain. But retirement changes everything. In retirement, there is no annual raise, no promotion, no increment to offset rising prices. Your income, at best, stays flat. Your expenses, however, keep climbing at that relentless 5%–6% every year.

WHEN INFLATION IS NOT EQUAL

What makes this even more insidious is that not all prices inflate at the same rate. If your holiday budget was ₹2 lakhs in 2019 and covered three domestic trips—budget airlines, three-star hotels, nothing extravagant—by 2025, you would need ₹3.5 lakhs for the exact same trips. Hotel rates in popular tourist destinations have nearly doubled. Flight prices during holiday seasons have become painful. Travel inflation in India has been running at close to 10% annually.

Medical expenses, however, are in a different category altogether. The monthly medical spend that was ₹8,000 in 2019 for routine checkups, medicines, and diagnostic tests is now ₹22,000 for the same items. The diabetes medication that cost ₹450 is now ₹950. Blood pressure pills went from ₹280 to ₹620, quarterly blood tests from ₹1,200 to ₹2,800, and a doctor's consultation fee from ₹800 to ₹1,600. Healthcare inflation in India has not been 5%. For many common medications, diagnostics, and procedures, the annual increase has been 8%–12%. And unlike travel, where you can choose to cut back on medical expenses, they are non-negotiable. You take the medicines or risk serious health consequences.

This is the key insight: you cannot use a single inflation number for retirement planning. If you travel extensively, your effective inflation might be 8%. If you have ongoing health conditions that require expensive medications, it might be 10%. You must think about your specific expense mix and plan accordingly. Assuming average inflation will apply to you is one of the most dangerous assumptions in retirement planning.

IS 2%–3% ABOVE INFLATION ENOUGH?

Let us return to Rajiv Malhotra. He had done his homework. His corpus was ₹1.5 crores. He needed ₹60,000 per month to maintain his lifestyle—₹7.2 lakhs per year. He had invested conservatively: 60% in fixed deposits and bonds earning 7%, 30% in equity mutual funds expected to return 11% over the long term, and 10% in gold. His weighted average return worked out to about 8.5% per year. With general inflation at 6%, he was beating it by 2.5%. The logic seemed sound. The mathematics appeared solid. But mathematics has a way of betraying us when we make the wrong assumptions.

Rajiv had assumed his ₹60,000 monthly expense would inflate at a uniform 6%. He had not accounted for the reality that his expense mix would change over time, with healthcare, the most expensive and fastest-inflating category, growing as a proportion of his total spending. Working through the numbers with that correction changes the picture entirely.

In year 1, his ₹7.2 lakh annual withdrawal represented 4.8% of his corpus. Assuming a slightly more optimistic 9% return, his corpus earned well and grew to ₹1.56 crores by year-end. By year 5, his annual expenses had grown to ₹9.1 lakhs, and his corpus had grown to ₹1.68 crores. Still manageable. By year 10, expenses were ₹11.8 lakhs, and the corpus had grown to ₹1.74 crores—the cushion was shrinking, but it was still there.

By year 15, at age 75, the trap snapped shut. His expenses had grown to ₹15.3 lakhs annually, more than double his starting figure. The corpus had peaked at ₹1.82 crores around year 12 and was now declining. Nine per cent returns were no longer enough to offset the growing withdrawals. By year 20, at age 80, his corpus was down to ₹1.1 crores, less than he had started with, while annual expenses were ₹19.9 lakhs. He was withdrawing 18% of his corpus each year just to meet basic expenses. By year 25, at age 85, his corpus was completely exhausted. He still needed ₹25.9 lakhs per year, but had nothing left.

Even beating inflation by 2%–3% per annum, you can still run out of money in the later years of retirement. The reason is straightforward: you need your returns to exceed not just inflation, but inflation plus your withdrawal rate.

This is the trap that catches so many retirees. Earning 2%–3% above inflation is sufficient only if you are not withdrawing from your corpus, if you are living entirely off returns, and the corpus itself is untouched. The moment you start drawing down your capital, which almost everyone must do in retirement, the mathematics changes completely. If you are withdrawing 5% of your corpus annually and inflation is running at 6%, you need returns of at least 11% just to stay even. Most retirees are not earning 11% safely. This means many retirees who feel comfortable today are on a slow path to running dry; they just do not see it yet because the deterioration is gradual. Year 1 looks fine. Year 5 looks fine. Year 10 feels tight but manageable. By year 15, the problem is obvious, but the options to fix it have dwindled dramatically.

HOW A SINGLE PERCENTAGE POINT CAN DESTROY A RETIREMENT PLAN

Here is an insight worth understanding deeply: small differences in inflation assumptions create enormous differences in outcomes over the length of a retirement.

Take two identical retirees. Both are 60 years old. Both have a ₹1 crore corpus. Both need ₹50,000 per month today, or ₹6 lakhs per year. Both expect to live to 90. Both earn 8% annually on their investments. The only difference: Retiree A assumes inflation at 5%; Retiree B assumes 6%. One percentage point. It sounds like splitting hairs.

After 10years, Retiree A's annual expenses have grown to ₹9.8 lakhs. Retiree B's to ₹10.7 lakhs—a gap of ₹90,000 per year. Noticeable, but not alarming. After 20 years, Retiree A needs ₹15.9 lakhs; Retiree B needs ₹19.2 lakhs—the gap has widened to ₹3.3 lakhs per year. Now it matters. After 30 years, at age 90, Retiree A needs ₹25.9 lakhs per year. Retiree B needs ₹34.4 lakhs per year—a difference of ₹8.5 lakhs, more than 40% higher. One percentage point of inflation difference, compounded over 30 years, produces a 40% difference in the income required to maintain the same lifestyle.

Put another way: if you assume 5% inflation and plan for a ₹1 crore corpus, but actual inflation turns out to be 6%, you should have started with ₹1.4 crores. That single percentage point error means you began 40% short of what you needed. The downside of being wrong is catastrophic. The upside of being conservative is merely that you end up with more money than you need, which is hardly a problem worth worrying about.

YOUR TURN: REVIEW SECTION 2 - LIFESTYLE & RISKS

This chapter is not meant to terrify you into paralysis. It is meant to replace complacency with honesty. Inflation is an enemy you can prepare for, but only if you are clear-eyed about the threat.

The goal of this exercise is not precision; nobody can predict the future exactly. The goal is to make you genuinely understand the scale of inflation's impact over a multi-decade retirement. Minor differences in assumptions create enormous differences in outcomes. Conservative assumptions protect you. Optimistic ones endanger you. Better to plan for 5% and experience four—you will have extra money. Far worse to plan for 4% and experience 5%—you will run out of money at 80 with potentially another decade to live.

THE GOOD NEWS: THREE PHASES, NOT ONE

If the numbers above have unsettled you, here is something genuinely reassuring: retirement is not a single uniform phase of 30 or 40 years. It has a distinct shape, and that shape works in your favour.

Think of retirement in three phases. The first are the Adventure Years—the initial years after you retire, when you are healthy, energetic, and determined to experience everything you have deferred during your working life. This is when bucket list spending is highest: international travel, family celebrations, hobbies requiring equipment or tuition, and the renovation you always planned. Spend this money. Spend it early, while you can enjoy it fully. The impact of inflation on bucket-list expenditure is minimal if you front-load it in the first decade.

The second phase is the Active Years—the middle stretch, where you have settled into a retirement routine. Local travel, social activities, family visits, and regular dining out. These are meaningful pleasures, but more predictable in cost and easier to manage. Discretionary spending is present but more controlled than in the Adventure Years.

The third phase is the Comfort Years—the later stage, typically from the late seventies onward, when consumption naturally slows. You travel less, entertain less, and spend less on most discretionary items. If your health holds, even medical costs can stay contained during this phase. Real expenses—the actual amount you spend, adjusted for what you actually consume—often drop meaningfully in the Comfort Years even as nominal prices continue to rise. The inflation threat is real, but your consumption base is also shrinking.

This phased reality provides a natural cushion. The years when your spending power is most vulnerable to inflation, your eighties and nineties, are also the years when your actual consumption tends to decline. The mathematics of retirement is still demanding, but it is less relentless than a single uniform projection suggests.

The second piece of good news is simpler: if you can generate even modest income in the early years of retirement—consulting work, advisory roles, part-time teaching, freelance projects—it reduces the pressure on your corpus precisely when that pressure is highest. Even funding 20% or 30% of your expenses through earned income in the first five to 10 years can dramatically improve your long-term position, because it allows your corpus to compound further before you begin drawing it down in earnest.

Your expenses will increase in nominal terms throughout retirement. But real consumption tends to fall as you age, particularly in the Comfort Years. Front-load your bucket list, stay partially engaged with work early in retirement, and let the phased structure of life itself work in your favour.

In the next chapter, we will work through a practical framework for managing your expenses across these three phases. The numbers are demanding, but they are manageable—if you face them honestly now.

10

A Practical Framework for Retirement Funding

Chapters 10 to 12 help you strengthen Section III: Income Sources & Retirement Corpus of your Desi Retirement Plan.

You've done the hard work. You've defined your core circle. You've quantified the major one-time expenses—education, weddings, and loans. You've broken down your lifestyle expenses in detail. You've built your three-layer healthcare defence. You've calculated what inflation will do to all these numbers over 20, 30, even 40 years.

Now you know what retirement will cost. Not the fantasy number you hoped for. The real number.

For most people, this number is significantly higher than they initially imagined. What started as "I need ₹60,000 per month" has become "I actually need ₹1,40,000 per month when I account for my parents, my children's upcoming needs, healthcare, social obligations, and inflation."

That's uncomfortable. But it's honest. And honesty is the only foundation for a plan that works.

Before we move forward to discuss your income sources and retirement preparedness, let me share with you a simple framework for thinking about how different types of expenses should be funded:

ESSENTIAL EXPENSES → PREDICTABLE INCOME

Your absolute essentials—housing, food, utilities, basic healthcare, and support to parents should ideally be covered by predictable income sources. Pension, rental income, annuities. Money that arrives regardless of market conditions.

Why? Because these expenses are non-negotiable. You can't skip paying rent or buying groceries because the stock market crashed 30%. These must be secure.

If your predictable income covers your core expenses, you have a foundation of security. Even in the worst market conditions, your basics are protected.

DESIRABLE EXPENSES → GROWTH-ORIENTED INCOME

Your extras—travel, entertainment, dining out, gifts, lifestyle upgrades—can be funded through investment withdrawals. These are flexible. If markets are down, you can cut back on travel. If your corpus is under stress, you can skip the expensive vacation.

This doesn't mean you're living in deprivation. It means you have the flexibility to adjust when needed without compromising your security.

ONE-TIME OBLIGATIONS (PROMISES) → EARMARKED CORPUS

Your children's education, weddings, and known medical procedures—these should be funded from specifically earmarked portions of your corpus, not from regular income or regular withdrawals.

You've already calculated these in previous chapters. That money is set aside. It's not available for anything else.

This way, even if markets dip or inflation accelerates, your essentials remain secure while lifestyle extras can be adjusted. You're not walking a financial tightrope. You have layers of protection.

WHY THIS MATTERS EMOTIONALLY

Planning expenses and income isn't just about numbers. It's about peace of mind.

Knowing that your household needs and medical bills are covered—regardless of market conditions—allows you to enjoy retirement. You're not checking your portfolio every morning with anxiety. You're not lying awake at 3 AM wondering if you'll run out of money.

Too often, retirees cut corners on their own happiness because they didn't plan properly. They have money, but they're terrified to spend it. They deny themselves simple pleasures—a nice meal out, a short trip, a gift for grandchildren, because they're not sure if it's "safe" to spend.

A structured approach avoids this trap. You know what's secure (covered by regular income). You know what's flexible (funded by corpus withdrawals). You know what's earmarked (one-time major expenses). Within this structure, you can spend confidently.

That confidence is worth more than any extra percentage point of return you might earn by taking on more risk.

Planning for retirement expenses is not about cutting down your dreams. It's about recognising your needs, preparing for surprises, and ensuring your lifestyle is sustainable.

Retirement should not feel like walking on a tightrope—one wrong step, and you fall. It should feel like a well-paved road where you know exactly what's coming ahead, where you've planned for the curves and the bumps, where you can enjoy the journey without constantly fearing you're about to run off the cliff.

You've built that road in this section of the book. You know your expenses. It's time to focus on the income sources that can help you fund your expenses.

11

Know Your Income Gap

You have estimated your expenses accurately in the previous chapters. Now, the most critical question: Where will this money come from?

Not all of it needs to come from your retirement corpus. Some of it will come from predictable income sources that continue after you retire. The gap between what you need and what these sources provide is what your retirement corpus must fund.

Understanding this gap is everything. It determines how much retirement corpus you need, what withdrawal rate is sustainable, and whether your retirement plan will work or fail.

THE TWO TYPES OF RETIREMENT INCOME

When you retire, money comes from two fundamentally different sources:

SOURCE 1: PREDICTABLE INCOME

This is money that arrives regularly, independent of your investment corpus. It doesn't depend on market performance. It doesn't require you to sell assets or withdraw from investments. It just... comes.

Examples:

- Pension from your employer or the government

- Rental income from property you own
- Part-time work or consulting income. I strongly recommend this, as it not only helps with your finances but also provides a sense of purpose, aids mental and emotional wellness, and keeps you socially engaged.

This income is predictable. You can count on it. It forms the foundation of your retirement cash flow.

In case you do not have any predictable income, you will have to rely entirely on the investment-derived income.

SOURCE 2: INVESTMENT-DERIVED INCOME

This is money you generate by withdrawing from your retirement corpus—your interest income earned from bank fixed deposits or bonds, dividends from stocks, systematic withdrawals from mutual funds, and from liquidating your financial assets.

This income depends entirely on your corpus size, your asset allocation, market performance, and how much you withdraw. It's the flexible portion. It's also the portion that can run out if you're not careful.

We define the income gap as the shortfall that needs to be funded from investments after reducing the predictable income from total annual expenses.

YOUR PREDICTABLE INCOME: WHAT ACTUALLY COUNTS?

Now let's figure out your predictable income. But first, a critical warning—be conservative here. It's tempting to inflate these numbers because they make your gap smaller and your situation look better. Resist that temptation.

PENSION:

If you're in a government job or a large corporate with a defined benefit pension plan, this is straightforward. Your pension amount is stated clearly. Use that number.

If you're in the private sector with no pension, this number is zero. Don't invent pension income you don't have.

If you're a professional or business owner, you likely have no pension unless you've specifically purchased an annuity plan. Be honest about this.

RENTAL INCOME:

Count only the net rental income after all costs—property tax, maintenance, repairs, vacancy periods. If your property generates ₹25,000 per month in rent but costs ₹8,000 per month to maintain, your net income is ₹17,000 per month.

If you own multiple properties, be realistic about vacancy rates. Two flats don't mean double income if one sits vacant for months while you search for tenants.

If you plan to sell a rental property and redeploy the capital into your retirement corpus, don't count rental income from that property. It's going to become part of your corpus, not a separate income stream.

PART-TIME WORK / CONSULTING:

This is the trickiest category because it involves assumptions about your future health, energy, market demand for your skills, and your own willingness to keep working.

Be conservative. If you think you could earn ₹5 lakhs per year consulting, budget ₹3 lakhs. If you think you could work for 10 years post-retirement, plan for 5 years. Health fails. Interest wanes. Markets change. Your skills become outdated. Don't build your entire retirement plan on optimistic assumptions about post-retirement income.

And critically: don't include this income if you're planning to "fully retire." If your dream retirement is zero work, don't count work income.

WHAT NOT TO COUNT:

This is critical. The following are NOT predictable income:

- Interest from fixed deposits (this comes from your corpus, already accounted for in investment returns)
- Annuities
- Your EPF corpus that you have not withdrawn yet
- Dividends from stocks or mutual funds (corpus-derived income)
- SWP from mutual funds (systematic withdrawal from corpus)
- "I'll sell some property when I need money" (that's corpus liquidation, not income)
- "My children will help me" (don't plan your retirement on your children's support)

If it comes from your investment corpus, it's investment-derived income, not predictable income. The distinction matters because we're trying to calculate the gap that your corpus must fill. Including corpus-derived income in "predictable income" double-counts and gives you false confidence.

Now you're ready to calculate your income gap:

STEP 1: WRITE DOWN YOUR ANNUAL EXPENSES

These are your expenses—your lifestyle expenses, your circle's needs, healthcare provisions, everything in today's terms.

Annual expenses (today): ₹_______

STEP 2: WRITE DOWN YOUR PREDICTABLE ANNUAL INCOME

Include only pension, rental income (net), and realistic part-time work.

Total Predictable Income: ₹_______ per year

STEP 3: CALCULATE YOUR INCOME GAP

Annual expenses: ₹_______

Minus predictable income: ₹_______

Is equal to the Income Gap: ₹_______ per year

This gap is the single most important number in your entire retirement plan. This is what your retirement corpus must generate, year after year, for 30–40 years.

In the next chapter, let us focus on what you have with you, as in your total investments. We will make the necessary adjustments to arrive at the retirement corpus.

12

What's Your Retirement Corpus?

Now that you have a clear idea about your income gap, do you have a retirement corpus that can fund that gap?

Most people would answer by pointing to their total investment assets. "I have ₹1.8 crores," they'd say. "That's my retirement corpus."

But that's not quite right. Not all of your ₹1.80 crore is available to generate retirement income. Some of it is already spoken for—earmarked for specific obligations that will arrive at specific times. You can't count money twice. You can't use the same rupee to fund your daughter's wedding *and* generate a monthly income.

This chapter helps you calculate your *actual* available retirement corpus—the money that's genuinely available to support you through 30–40 years of retirement.

YOUR STARTING POINT: TOTAL INVESTMENT ASSETS

Begin with the number you calculated in Chapter 3—your total investible assets across all categories: debt, equities, precious metals, and real estate.

Total Investment Assets: ₹_______

This is everything you have that could theoretically fund your retirement. Now let's see what's available.

THE THREE ESSENTIAL DEDUCTIONS

Not all your investment assets are available for retirement income. Three categories of money must be set aside first:

DEDUCTION 1: PROMISES TO FAMILY & SELF

You calculated these in detail in an earlier chapter: your children's education expenses, their wedding expenses, outstanding loans you'll pay off at retirement, and other major family obligations.

These amounts must be earmarked now, even if these expenses are several years away. This money has a specific job to do. It's not available for generating retirement income.

Total Promises: ₹_______

DEDUCTION 2: HEALTHCARE BUFFER

You built your three-layer healthcare defence in an earlier chapter—the dedicated fund meant specifically to cover insurance gaps, OPD expenses, and medical emergencies.

This buffer protects you from having to liquidate your retirement corpus at the worst possible time when a medical crisis strikes. It sits separately in liquid, accessible instruments.

From your healthcare planning:

Healthcare Buffer: ₹_______

YOUR RETIREMENT CORPUS: THE CALCULATION

Now, calculate your actual available retirement corpus:

Total Investment Assets: ₹_______

Less: Promises to Family/Self: ₹_______

Less: Healthcare Buffer: ₹_______

Is Equal To: Retirement Corpus: ₹_______

This is the money available to generate income for 30–40 years of retirement expenses. Not your total assets. Your retirement corpus.

IF YOU'RE STILL WORKING: ADDING FUTURE SAVINGS

If you're reading this several years before retirement, your current retirement corpus isn't your final number. You'll continue saving, and your existing corpus will grow.

Here's how to account for that:

Current retirement corpus (after all deductions): ₹_______

Years until retirement: _______

Additional savings each year until retirement: ₹_______

Total additional savings (years × annual savings): ₹_______

Growth on current investment corpus at __% p.a. for ___ years: ₹_______ (Use any online compound interest calculator—I have provided the factors in Annexure-II)

Savings in SIP (these grow too as you add them): ₹_______ (This is slightly more complex. Use a SIP calculator online—I have provided the factors in Annexure-III)

Inflows for maturity of insurance policies/inheritance: ₹_______

Total Retirement Corpus (At Retirement): ₹_______

If you're within 1–2 years of retirement or already retired, skip this section. Your current corpus is essentially your final corpus.

YOUR TURN: COMPLETE SECTION 3: REVIEW INCOME SOURCES AND RETIREMENT CORPUS.

You've completed the most important calculation in retirement planning. You know what you have available—not your total assets, but your genuine retirement corpus after all obligations are accounted for.

Some of you discovered your corpus is comfortable. Some found it's tight but workable. Some, like Ajay, found it insufficient and requires significant action.

Whatever your number, you now have clarity. Not comfortable clarity perhaps, but honest clarity. And honesty is the only foundation for decisions that work.

The number might not be what you hoped for. You might wish you'd started earlier, saved more, and made different choices.

But you can't fix what you can't see. And now you can see clearly.

In the next chapter, we'll determine what these numbers mean for your retirement readiness.

Turn the page. Let's assess where you stand.

13

Know Your AWR. Know Your Future

Chapters 13 and 14 help you strengthen Section 4: Your Retirement Preparedness of the Desi Retirement Plan.

There is an uncomfortable truth that nobody tells you about retirement planning: You will only know, with absolute certainty, whether your plan truly worked on the last day of your life.

Until then, you are living with assumptions. How long will you live? What will inflation do to your expenses? Will markets cooperate or confound you? Will there be a medical emergency in year 12, a family obligation in year 20? Every projection you make rests on answers to questions that life has not yet provided.

No wonder most retirees carry a quiet anxiety. Not about next year, that feels manageable, but about the final years. The years when there is no room for error, no time to recover, and no ability to return to work. The years when a failing plan reveals itself too late to be fixed.

You deserve better than that. You deserve to know not at the end, but now, and every single year, whether your plan is on track.

What you need is not a complicated model or a stack of portfolio statements. You need one clear number that tells you whether you're doing fine or whether it's time to make changes.

THAT NUMBER IS YOUR ANNUAL WITHDRAWAL RATE (AWR).

AWR is the percentage of your retirement corpus you withdraw in the first year of retirement to cover your income gap: the expenses that your fixed-income sources, pension, rental income, and the like, do not cover.

The formula

AWR = (Income Gap ÷ Retirement Corpus) × 100

Income Gap ₹ _______ (from Chapter 10)

Retirement Corpus ₹ _______ (from Chapter 11)

Your AWR _______ %

The concept has its roots in western financial research. In the 1990s, American planner William Bengen showed that retirees drawing 4% annually from a diversified portfolio could expect their money to last 30 years through most market conditions, the origin of the widely cited "4% Rule."

But India is not America. Our inflation runs higher. Our markets behave differently. Our family structures carry obligations that western models never account for. The 4% Rule offers a useful starting point, not a finished answer. Desi retirement demands its own framework.

That framework is built around three ranges:

RANGE I · BELOW 3%: *THE LEGACY BUILDER*

If your AWR is below 3%, you have not merely planned for retirement—you have built something that will likely outlast you by decades, potentially supporting the next generation as well.

Your corpus can sustain your lifestyle with significant room to spare. Market downturns will not materially threaten your plan. You can support your family generously without compromising your own security.

Your goal

Preserve what you have built. You have already won. The only meaningful risk now is an unforced error, a concentrated bet, a product you do not understand, or the temptation to chase higher returns you do not need.

What to do

- Diversify across asset classes and geographies -concentration is the enemy of a legacy portfolio.
- Build a written list of what you will not invest in and follow it without exception. Real estate often belongs here: rental yields are low, and property requires active management in the years when you want the least of it.
- Increase your obligations to yourself. You have earned this retirement. Live it.
- Begin thinking about tax-efficient wealth transfer while you still have the time and clarity to do it well.

RANGE II · 3% TO 5%: *THE GOLD STANDARD*

A withdrawal rate between 3% and 5% is the sweet spot of desi retirement. Your corpus can weather market crashes, absorb unexpected expenses, and still sustain your lifestyle across three to four decades. You are comfortable without being careless, and secure without being overexposed.

You are in good shape. But good shape is not the same as invincible. Market timing matters. Spending discipline matters. Your asset allocation needs active maintenance through bull markets and downturns alike.

What your portfolio needs

- A balanced mix: roughly 50%–55% Debt, 35%–40% Equity, 5%–10% Precious metals.

- Two to three years of expenses in liquid, easily accessible instruments. Your buffer against needing to sell equity at the wrong moment.
- Systematic rebalancing so your allocation does not drift during strong markets.
- A tax-efficient withdrawal strategy, because how you draw down matters as much as how much you draw down.
- What to watch for
- Do not inflate your lifestyle simply because you can afford to. Lifestyle creep is silent and cumulative.
- Do not panic-sell equity during corrections. Your buffer exists precisely so you do not have to.
- Do not take on unplanned family obligations without stress-testing your plan first.

A note for those at 4%–5%

You are at the upper end of the gold standard. Still safe but with less margin. Consider keeping three years of expenses in liquid funds rather than two, holding equity at 35% rather than 40%, and setting aside a small portion of income each year as a precautionary buffer. The discipline you maintain now is what keeps you firmly inside this range a decade from now.

RANGE III · ABOVE 5%: *THE WARNING ZONE*

Above 5%, your corpus is depleting faster than it can be sustainably replenished. You are not necessarily in crisis, but you are on a path that leads there. One significant market downturn, one unexpected expense, and manageable discomfort become a genuine hardship.

The urgency of the response depends on how far above 5% you are.

5%–6%: Course correction needed

You are managing, but only just. The corrections required are uncomfortable, not catastrophic, and they are far more effective now than in five years when the problem has compounded.

- Reduce spending on desirables by 10%–15%, particularly during market downturns.
- Consider working part-time or consulting work in the early years of retirement.
- Defer major purchases and large family commitments where possible.

6%–8%: Serious action required

Your corpus is depleting at a dangerous pace. The adjustments needed are significant, and the delay makes each one harder.

- Cut expenses now, not eventually.
- Return to work if physically possible—even part-time income meaningfully changes the trajectory.
- Consider downsizing your home if it would free up substantial capital.
- Have an honest conversation with family about what support you can and cannot provide.

Above 8%: Fundamental restructuring

At this level, the plan as it stands is not sustainable. This is not a moment for minor adjustments—it is a moment for clear-eyed decisions about how you live, where you live, and what you earn.

- Return to full-time or substantial work, if possible.
- Consider relocating to a significantly lower-cost environment—your hometown, a Tier 2 or Tier 3 city.
- Sell assets that are not generating income.

- ▲ If living with adult children is feasible, set aside pride and evaluate it honestly. A difficult conversation today is far better than a financial collapse in year 15.

MYTH: LARGER RETIREMENT CORPUS = BETTER RETIREMENT PREPAREDNESS

Here is something that surprises most people when they first encounter it. Here is an example of two individuals:

Individual A: ₹5 crore corpus; Annual Withdrawal: ₹35 lakhs; AWR: 7%

Individual B: ₹2 crore corpus; Annual withdrawal: ₹7 lakhs;

AWR: 3.5%

Guess who is in trouble and who is ok?

The individual with the larger corpus is in trouble. The individual with a smaller corpus is in better shape because retirement readiness is about the relationship between what you have and what you need.

The person withdrawing ₹35 lakhs annually will watch their corpus erode steadily through every market downturn, with limited ability to recover. The person withdrawing ₹7 lakhs can invest patiently, wait out corrections, and let compounding do its work across decades.

REALITY: RETIREMENT CORPUS SIZE IS NOT THE MEASURE OF RETIREMENT READINESS. AWR IS.

Your Assumptions Matter

The AWR is only as reliable as the assumptions behind it. For desi retirement, those assumptions should be grounded in Indian reality, not optimistic projections or western benchmarks.

Assume inflation at 5%–6% per year, and not 4%, which has historically underestimated what Indian households experience.

Assume investment returns of 8%–10% p.a. for a balanced portfolio—achievable with discipline but not guaranteed. And plan for a time horizon of 35 to 40 years. People are living longer. The cost of running out of money at 85 is far greater than the cost of being slightly more conservative at 65.

With these assumptions, the research and experience of Indian market conditions point to the same conclusion:

Below 3%, you are building a legacy.

3%–5% is the zone where retirement plans hold.

Above 5%, you are borrowing against a future that may not cooperate.

Think of your corpus as a tank of water on your rooftop. The AWR is the tap. Open it too wide and the tank empties before the monsoon arrives. Manage the flow carefully, and it sustains you through every dry season ahead.

Your job is to set the right flow—not so little that you feel deprived, not so much that you run out. For most desi retirees, that means finding your way to 3%–5% and staying there.

If you are already in that range, you are prepared. If you are below it, you are more than prepared. And if you are above it, the next chapter is written for you—5 specific strategies to bring your AWR down to where it needs to be, whether you need a minor adjustment or a significant course correction.

Compute your number. Then let it guide you.

14

Five Strategies to Improve Your Retirement Preparedness

You have calculated your AWR. You know which range you are in. Now comes the question that matters: what can you do about it? If you are already in a safe zone, this chapter helps you stay there. If your AWR is above 5%, this chapter shows you how to move towards safety, not through wishful thinking, but through six concrete interventions, each of which you can begin acting on today.

Before we go through the strategies, do one quick calculation. Write down your current AWR from the previous chapter, decide on your target, and calculate the gap. Every strategy in this chapter is aimed at closing that gap.

Current AWR: ________%

Target AWR: __________%

Gap to Close: ________%

The gap tells you the scale of the work ahead. A gap of 1% is manageable with modest adjustments. A gap of 3% or more needs a combination of strategies working together. The good news is that these strategies compound; each one you deploy makes the others more effective.

STRATEGY 1: WORK A FEW MORE YEARS

If you are within five to 10 years of your planned retirement and your AWR is uncomfortably high, this is often the single most powerful intervention available. Every additional year you work does three things at once: you add fresh savings to your corpus, your existing corpus continues growing, and you delay withdrawals, giving the whole sum more time to compound. The mathematics are dramatic. A 58-year-old with a ₹1.5 crore corpus and a ₹20 lakh annual income gap carries an AWR of 13.3%, which is dangerously high. If they work three more years and save ₹8 lakhs annually, their corpus grows to ₹2.12 crores, and their AWR falls to 9.4%. Still high, but a significant move in the right direction.

Indian corporate culture often forces retirement at 58 or 60, but that is not the only way to generate income. Consulting in your field, advisory roles, teaching, freelance work for smaller firms—these are not second-best options. For many professionals, the transition years between full employment and full retirement turn out to be the most intellectually rewarding of their careers. The question to ask yourself is not whether you can sustain a 40-hour work week until 65. The question is whether you can generate meaningful income in some form for three to five more years. If the honest answer is yes, this strategy alone may solve a large part of your problem.

STRATEGY 2: REDUCE YOUR EXPENSES

Nobody wants to hear this. You have worked hard, and you deserve to enjoy retirement. But if your AWR is above 5%, your current expense level is mathematically unsustainable. You have two choices: reduce expenses now voluntarily or have them reduced for you involuntarily when your corpus runs dry in your mid-seventies. The first option gives you dignity and control. The second gives you neither.

The place to start is your desirable expenses—travel, dining, entertainment, gifts, lifestyle upgrades, not your essentials. If your AWR is between 5% and 7%, trimming desirable expenses by 10%–15% will often bring you to safety. That is not deprivation. That is discipline. The harder conversation is around family obligations: reducing support to children feels unfair, cutting festival spending feels like losing face, and pulling back on helping parents feels cruel. But becoming financially dependent on your children in your seventies because you overspent in your sixties is worse for everyone. Have the honest conversation now, while you still have choices.

STRATEGY 3: GENERATE PART-TIME INCOME IN RETIREMENT

Part-time work in retirement is not a consolation prize for those who did not save enough. For many people, it becomes the most fulfilling dimension of their retirement years. You stay engaged with the world, your health and mental sharpness benefit, and the income, even if modest, has a disproportionate impact on your AWR by reducing the burden on your corpus.

Indian business culture has a particular advantage here: experience is respected. Retired professionals find genuine demand for their knowledge as advisers to small businesses, mentors at colleges, independent consultants, or freelance specialists. This is not going back to work. This is staying relevant while getting paid for it.

STRATEGY 4: DELAY OR REDUCE MAJOR ONE-TIME EXPENSES

Go back to Section 1 of your plan where you captured the promises you made to others and yourself. If your AWR is uncomfortably high, those numbers deserve a second look. Can your child take an education loan for part of their fees rather than drawing entirely from your corpus? Can the wedding be meaningful without being extravagant? Can the Europe trip wait three years while your corpus continues to grow? These are not easy questions, and there are no universal answers. But the mathematics are worth understanding. If you reduce committed one-time obligations from ₹1.1 crores to ₹80 lakhs, you free ₹30 lakhs for your retirement corpus. If your corpus was ₹1.17 crores, it becomes ₹1.47 crores, a 25% increase that directly improves your AWR.

Most families, when approached honestly, understand. The conversation most people avoid is the one that would help. Set a firm number, explain your situation, and let the family work within that boundary. You are not abandoning your obligations. You are being responsible about the limits of what you can sustain.

STRATEGY 5: OPTIMISE YOUR INVESTMENT PORTFOLIO

Two retirees with identical corpus, identical expenses, and identical withdrawal rates can have entirely different outcomes depending purely on how they invest. A well-managed portfolio earning 9% versus a carelessly managed one earning 7% may seem like a modest difference, but over 30 years on a ₹1 crore corpus, that gap produces ₹13.3 crores against ₹7.6 crores. If your AWR is 5%–6%, improving your investment returns by even 1% may close your gap entirely without touching your expenses or your plans.

The most common mistakes are predictable: parking everything in fixed deposits whose real return after inflation is near zero, holding too much equity near retirement, panicking when markets fall, concentrating in a single asset class, and making emotional decisions that lock in losses at the worst possible moment. Optimising your portfolio does not mean chasing higher returns at greater risk. It means proper asset allocation for your age and income needs, genuine diversification, systematic rebalancing, and the behavioural discipline to stay the course when markets test you. The entire next section of this book is dedicated to exactly this—how to build and manage an investment portfolio that generates sustainable income for 30– 40 years.

No single strategy will transform your retirement preparedness overnight. But two or three of them, deployed together, almost always can. The most important step is to be honest with yourself about which one applies to your situation and then act.

Go back to Section 4 of your plan. List the strategies you will pursue. Assign a target improvement to each. Add them up. If the combined improvement closes your AWR gap, you have your plan. If it does not, go back and be more ambitious. The numbers do not lie, but they also do not judge. They simply tell you what needs to change and by how much.

PART - III

BUILDING A RESILIENT RETIREMENT PORTFOLIO

15

Back to Basics

Section III: Building a Resilient Retirement Portfolio and Section IV: The Desi Investment Products help you strengthen Section 5: Optimising investments for Retirement of your Desi Retirement Plan.

Investments is a subject by itself, and I felt that it would be useful if I could provide a meaningful perspective to help you invest with confidence.

Indian equities have been extraordinarily generous to those who stayed invested. Over the past two decades, patient investors have seen their money grow in ways that would have seemed improbable at the start. If you are approaching retirement today with a substantial corpus, chances are that equity has done most of the heavy lifting. It is natural, then, to carry that confidence forward—to assume that what worked during your earning years will continue to work through your retirement.

But here is where the story quietly changes.

During your working years, time was on your side. A sharp market fall was an opportunity, not a crisis. You had income coming in, years ahead of you, and the luxury of simply waiting for recovery. In retirement, that buffer disappears. Now you are drawing from the portfolio, not adding to it. A 40% fall does not just shrink your corpus—it shrinks it at the very moment you need it to last. And if you sell in panic, as many do, you lock in those losses permanently. The market may recover. Your plan may not.

The last 20 years of the Indian equity markets were remarkable. But the next 30 years of your retirement will test something different entirely—not your ability to grow wealth, but your ability to protect it steadily, systematically, across decades that will include crises you cannot predict and recoveries that will feel far too slow.

*A **resilient retirement portfolio** is not the one that grows the fastest in good times. It is the one that holds together across time.*

It grows steadily, protects you from severe setbacks, and allows you to draw income without constant anxiety.

To hold together across time, a portfolio needs more than good investments. It needs structure. It needs to be built around a clear understanding of who you are as an investor, what you are trying to achieve, and what is realistic. Six ideas determine whether your portfolio will support you through the decades ahead or quietly let you down.

THE SIX IDEAS

One: *Asset allocation:* Before you choose a single investment, you need to decide how to divide your money across equity, debt, and other assets. This one decision shapes almost everything that follows. It determines how much you grow in good times and how much you fall in bad ones. Over long periods, getting this right matters far more than picking the "right" fund or the "right" stock. Most investors focus relentlessly on selection. The more important question is proportion.

Two: *Investment biases and behaviour*

Every investor carries invisible weight—beliefs shaped by experience, personality, and memory. If equity markets have rewarded you generously in the past, you likely hold more equity than is prudent. When markets correct sharply, that excess exposure becomes a source of panic rather than patience. If real estate has been your anchor, concentration and illiquidity follow. You are asset-rich, cash-poor, and completely unprepared when retirement demands liquidity.

These biases are not character flaws. But left unexamined, they become the single most reliable way to derail a retirement plan.

Three: *Realistic returns and drawdowns*

Many retirement plans look flawless on paper because they assume generous returns. Reality is rarely that cooperative. A strong plan is built on expectations you can count on, not ones that merely feel good to project.

Equally important is the question of drawdowns—how far can your portfolio fall from its peak? The "Nifty50 index" fell by over 60% during the 2008 global financial crisis. Because such moments are rare, most investors treat them as distant abstractions. They are not.

A 10% fall is uncomfortable.

A 30% fall tests your resolve.

A 60% fall can break it entirely.

The deeper the fall, the longer the recovery—financially and emotionally. Knowing your tolerance for drawdown is not pessimism. It is preparation.

Four: *Your investment objective statement*

What, precisely, are you trying to achieve? This sounds like a simple question. It rarely has a simple answer. Return and risk exist in permanent tension—higher ambitions expose you to greater volatility, while excessive caution leaves you vulnerable to inflation over time. A well-constructed investment objective finds the balance: realistic returns, manageable drawdowns, a sustainable withdrawal rate, and tax efficiency—so that your expenses are funded in real terms, and your corpus continues to grow alongside inflation. Without this statement, every investment decision is made in a vacuum.

Five: *Concentration*

A portfolio built around a few concentrated bets can perform brilliantly for a while. The hidden cost is fragility. When those bets go wrong, there is nothing else to hold the structure up. Diversification rarely feels exciting. It almost never produces the highest return in any given year. What it consistently does is prevent catastrophic loss. And in retirement, avoiding catastrophic loss is more valuable than chasing the highest possible gain.

Six: *Your assumptions*

Tie everything together, and you arrive here: the numbers underlying your entire plan. What returns are you expecting? What rate of inflation? What will you spend each year, and how might that change? These assumptions are the foundation. If they are too optimistic, the plan looks robust today and fails quietly later—precisely when you can least afford it. The most dangerous retirement plan is one that works on a spreadsheet but was never built to survive reality.

Taken individually, each of these ideas seems manageable. Together, they determine whether your retirement holds or fractures under pressure.

The goal is not to eliminate risk. That is neither possible nor desirable. It is to manage risk in a way that allows your plan to endure different market conditions and phases of life, even through the moments when your instincts are loudest and most likely to mislead you.

Retirement is not a short journey. For many people, it spans 25, even 30 years. Over such a horizon, the investors who fare best are rarely the ones who took the most risk. They are the ones who managed it well, stayed disciplined, and above all, avoided the large mistakes.

A strong retirement portfolio is not built on optimism. It is built on clarity, balance, and the willingness to hold steady when everything inside you says otherwise.

In the chapters that follow, we will examine each of these six ideas in depth—not to make you an expert in financial theory, but to give you a portfolio you genuinely understand. One you trust enough to stay with.

That trust, as it turns out, is the most valuable asset you can own.

16

Asset Allocation – The Holy Grail of Investing

Managing your retirement corpus is the vital link that ensures that your money lasts in your retirement years. This is a vast and complex subject. Also, there are tonnes of jargon that make it very confusing. What I have attempted here is to minimise the jargon and focus your attention on the most crucial elements of your investment plan.

As you would have noticed, the subject of investments is divided into two parts. In the first part, we focus on the structure of your portfolio as the biggest mistakes happen due to this reason. The second part discusses the products so that you get a grip on how best to construct your ideal investment portfolio. For those of you who have a good amount of investment experience and/or expertise, you can skip the section related to products.

Before we go ahead with a discussion of investments, I would like to reiterate that the examples I am sharing here are meant only for learning purposes. Nothing that I share here constitutes investment advice. Please consult your investment adviser before making any changes to your investment portfolio.

When it comes to managing money in retirement, many people feel lost in a maze of financial jargon. Terms like "asset allocation," "debt instruments," or "diversification" sound like they belong in a finance textbook, not in a retiree's living room.

But here's the good news: you don't need to master all the jargon. You only need to understand one key idea: Asset Allocation.

This single concept can make the difference between worrying about your money and feeling truly confident about your financial future.

Let's begin by simplifying what it means.

WHAT IS AN ASSET CLASS?

An asset class is simply a group of investments that behave similarly.

Think of your money as being divided into **four buckets**, each serving a specific purpose:

Debt – for safety, liquidity, and steady income

Equities – for growth and inflation protection

Precious metals – for diversification and emotional comfort

Real estate – for diversification and steady income

Each bucket has its own personality—how much it can earn, how much risk it carries, and how easy it is to access your money. By mixing these wisely, you create a plan that can withstand market ups and downs.

DEBT - THE SAFETY, LIQUIDITY, AND STEADY INCOME BUCKET

This is your **comfort fund**—money you can access quickly for emergencies or short-term expenses. It's low-risk, offers modest returns, and keeps your cash within easy reach. We can further categorise debt into short-term or long-term. To keep things simple, I have clubbed them under the debt category.

EXAMPLES OF SHORT-TERM DEBT PRODUCTS:

- Savings accounts
- Fixed deposits (under 3 years)
- Post Office Time Deposits
- Liquid Funds
- Short-Term Debt Funds
- Treasury Bills
- Short-term government or corporate bonds

The risks that are associated with these investments include:

- *Inflation risk*: Returns may not beat inflation.
- *Reinvestment risk*: Future deposit rates could fall.

EXAMPLES OF LONG-TERM DEBT PRODUCTS:

- Senior Citizen Savings Scheme (SCSS)
- Post Office Monthly Income Scheme (POMIS)
- RBI Floating Rate Bonds
- Government Bonds or G-Secs
- Bank Fixed Deposits (3–10 years)
- Company Deposits (from reputed, AAA-rated firms)
- Debt Mutual Funds (Corporate Bond Funds, Gilt Funds, Medium Duration Funds)
- Annuities from insurance companies

The key risk associated with these investments is:

Interest rate risk: Value may fall if rates rise.

Credit risk: This refers to the risk that you may not receive the principal amount.

EQUITIES - THE GROWTH AND INFLATION-PROTECTION BUCKET

Equities are your **growth engine**. They help your money grow faster than inflation and ensure that your wealth doesn't lose value over time.

In simple terms, when you invest in equities, you're owning a small part of a business. As the business grows, your share in it becomes more valuable.

EXAMPLES OF EQUITY PRODUCTS:

- Direct shares of listed companies
- Equity Mutual Funds (large-cap, flexi-cap, multi-cap)
- Index Funds (Nifty 50, Sensex, etc.)
- Equity Portfolio Management Services (PMS)

The biggest risk while investing in equities is:

Market risk: Prices can fluctuate sharply in the short term.

Liquidity Risk: Unlisted and small-cap stocks have generally lower liquidity.

PRECIOUS METALS – THE DIVERSIFICATION AND EMOTIONAL BUCKET

Gold, Silver, Platinum, etc., are all examples of this category. They provide diversification and emotional comfort. However, they also come with their own challenges. You can hold them in physical form or through investment products that mimic their prices. For example, Gold ETF / Sovereign Gold Bonds

The key risks include:

Volatility: Gold and silver prices can swing sharply.

Storage: You need lockers or other means to store them safely.

REAL ESTATE – FOR DIVERSIFICATION AND REGULAR INCOME

Real Estate has been the favourite of Indian investors. We generally do not include the primary residence in investment calculations. If you own residential or commercial real estate that you plan to rent out, it is included in your investment plan. Land, agricultural or otherwise, is included here. REITs too would get included as part of your real estate investments, though you may buy them as you buy stocks. The investment returns of this asset class are from capital appreciation and rental income.

The risks associated with real estate, apart from market risks, include:

Liquidity: They are not easy to buy or sell.

Maintenance: There could be significant costs associated with the maintenance of properties.

Legal Title: Many real estate investments get entangled in legal title issues.

BRINGING IT ALL TOGETHER - ASSET ALLOCATION

Now that you understand the four buckets, the next question is: How much should you put into each one?

That mix—your asset allocation—is the single most important decision you'll make about your money. It determines your balance between income, growth, and safety. We will discuss the ideal asset allocation in a later chapter.

THE FINAL WORD

Understanding asset classes and asset allocation is like learning how to balance on a bicycle—once you get it, everything else becomes easy.

You don't have to be an expert in markets or economics. You just need to know—Where your money is parked, why it's there, and what role it plays in your financial peace of mind.

That clarity alone can transform anxiety into confidence.

So, if there's one concept—one piece of financial jargon—that every retiree must understand, it's this: **Asset Allocation.**

Because in the long run, it's not about how much you earn from a single investment; it's about how wisely you spread your money across all of them.

17

Identifying Your Investment Biases

In the previous chapter, we discussed the concept of asset classes at length. The way your investments are spread across the buckets is termed asset allocation. In this chapter, we will understand your investment biases based on your asset allocation.

Let me start the discussion by describing the different kinds of investors, what their asset allocations reflect, and the risks they carry from a retirement perspective.

THE REAL ESTATE KING:

The real estate king has achieved great success with their investments. The formula for growth has been to borrow and invest in real estate. Their investment portfolio is largely built around a few properties. With a real-estate-heavy portfolio, the biggest casualty generally is liquidity. You are asset-rich but liquidity-poor.

The asset allocation pattern of the Real Estate King will typically be:

Debt: 5%–10%

Equities: 5%–10%

Precious Metals: 5%–10%

Real Estate: 70%–85%

THE CAUTIOUS RETIREE:

The cautious retiree has had a terrible experience investing in equity markets and, as a result, they swear against investing in equities. The cautious retiree has a portfolio built around fixed deposits, annuities, and bonds.

The risk that you create with this approach is that of the silent killer: inflation. By the time you realise this, it is generally too late.

The asset allocation pattern of a cautious retiree would be:

Debt: 80%–90%

Equities: 0%–5%

Precious Metals: 0%–5%

Real Estate: 0%

THE OPTIMIST RETIREE:

The mantra of the optimist retiree is that equities are the best long-term bet. Such an individual will have a portfolio that mainly consists of direct equity and equity-oriented mutual funds. They are the ones who have had great success with investing through Systematic Investment Plans.

The risk for such an investor is that equities do not go up in a straight line. An equity-heavy portfolio will go through shallow and deep corrections. The recovery period could last from a few days to a few months, and many investors, especially in countries like Japan, have found that it can sometimes take decades to return to the highest level they experienced in the equity markets. The risk is that if they panic during downturns or must liquidate during stressful periods in the market, they would never be able to get back the valuation, though equity markets may eventually grow back to newer highs.

Debt: 5%–15%

Equities: 65%–80%

Precious metals: 0%–5%

Real Estate: 0%

THE ESOP RETIREE:

The concentration trap is applicable across equity, debt, and real estate. Let me illustrate the risk for investors with skewed portfolios due to exposure to stock options.

The ESOP Retiree was fortunate to be employed with companies that did extremely well in their lifetimes. If you have made money through stock options, it is likely that a single stock or a few stocks dominate your equity portfolio. The challenge, however, is that they are unable to accept that there can be a downside risk associated with this kind of portfolio. This is due to what we term as anchoring bias. They anchor their expectations to the great growth that they have witnessed in that stock in the past.

There are innumerable examples in the stock market where individuals' entire portfolios were wiped out for this reason. Enron was one of the greatest companies in its time in the USA. There are stories where not only did people who worked there lose their jobs, but they also lost their entire retirement savings, as they had invested all their money in Enron stock.

If ESOPs have worked for someone, their overall portfolio is likely to be dominated by a single stock. And the holding could typically be 75% or more of their overall portfolio. If someone is big into real estate, a single investment could account for 90% of their portfolio. Never a good idea to be so concentrated in a single investment.

THE INFLATION-ERA RETIREE:

Last but not least are your investment return assumptions that you expect from the markets. It is difficult to anticipate what kind of changes you are likely to experience due to economic and market-related events. Who would have visualised a zero-interest rate regime in several countries in Europe? Closer home, India was a high-inflation economy till 2000. Then things changed, inflation was brought under control, and as a result, the investment returns in equity markets have also dropped since then. But for the ones who experienced the heady returns of a high-inflation economy, expect similar returns going forward as well.

India witnessed a very high inflation rate in the 1980s and 1990s. Investors who witnessed that era tend to anchor their investment expectations to the returns it generated back then. They would expect equities to deliver 15% p.a. and debt to deliver 9% p.a.–10% p.a. on a consistent basis. The reality is that inflation rates have come down, and so are the likely returns from equities and debt in the future.

Your investment biases lead to the biggest mistakes in your investments. These mistakes don't happen all at once. They compound over the years. And by the time the damage becomes visible—often at age 70 or 75—there's very little that can be done. You can't go back to work. You can't take on more risk to "catch up." You can't undo a decade of poor decisions.

18

Defining the Right Investment Goals

Before you decide which mutual fund to buy or which stock to pick, you need to be clear about your investment goals. So, what is it that you are trying to accomplish with your investments? Generic answers like *"I want to safeguard my money"* or *"I want the highest possible returns"* are not useful. They sound good, but they don't help you make decisions.

Your investment returns must do two things simultaneously—generate enough income for your expenses and protect your corpus from inflation.

Here's the math. If you need to withdraw 4% of your corpus annually to meet expenses, and inflation is running at 5%, your investments need to earn at least 9% per year just to stay even. Miss this target consistently, and your corpus starts shrinking in real terms.

This may seem simplistic, but it is quite powerful. If you get this right, your retirement corpus does not deplete in real terms. In fact, even after meeting your annual expenses, it continues to grow at least at the rate of inflation. So, the minimum return that you need to generate from your retirement corpus is the sum of your withdrawal rate and the rate of inflation.

Your first investment goal, therefore, is simple: earn a return that keeps your corpus ahead of inflation, even after withdrawals.

In retirement, returns are only one side of the story; risk matters just as much. And the biggest mistakes are not made in normal times—they happen when markets are at extremes. You will face these situations at least once every 7 to 10 years. Your ability to stick to your plan depends on how much loss you can tolerate without panicking.

My preferred way of looking at risk is through **drawdowns**—the percentage fall in your portfolio from its peak to its lowest point. If your portfolio was worth ₹1 crore and drops to ₹80 lakhs, that's a 20% drawdown.

Here's what different drawdowns feel like:

10% Drawdown (₹1 crore → ₹90 lakhs)

Uncomfortable, but manageable, happens almost every year; most investors can live with this

20% Drawdown (₹1 crore → ₹80 lakhs)

Seriously unsettling, happens every 3–4 years, this is where panic begins

30–40% Drawdown (₹1 crore → ₹60–70 lakhs)

Emotionally draining, it occurs once or twice a decade, and many investors make poor decisions here

50%+ Drawdown (₹1 crore → ₹50 lakhs or below)

Extreme stress, rare, but possible, very few investors stay invested through this.

Ask yourself honestly: if your ₹1 crore portfolio falls to ₹80 lakhs in three months, would you stay calm and stick to your plan, get nervous but hold steady, or panic and exit?

If the honest answer is the third option, then you need a portfolio with lower expected drawdowns, even if it means accepting lower returns.

There is another dimension to drawdowns that often gets ignored—the time it takes. A 10% fall may seem manageable, but if that fall happens slowly over three years and then takes another two years to recover, that's five years of zero returns.

Even shallow drawdowns can feel painful if they stretch over long periods. It's not just about how much your portfolio falls but also how long it takes to recover.

Your second investment goal is clear: build a portfolio whose drawdowns you can live through.

There is one more risk that most investors completely ignore: the **sequence of returns**. Two investors can earn the same average return over time and still end up with very different outcomes. This becomes critical in retirement, when you are making withdrawals.

Consider this: two investors start with ₹1 crore and withdraw ₹5 lakhs every year. Both earn an average return of 9% over 10 years, but their sequences differ. Investor A faces negative returns in the first few years and positive returns later, while Investor B enjoys strong returns initially and faces declines later. Despite the same average return, Investor A ends up with a much lower corpus.

Why does this happen? Because losses in the early years hurt more—your portfolio is larger, and you are also withdrawing from it at the same time. This is called **sequence of returns risk**.

Your third investment goal is therefore: **protect your portfolio in the early years of retirement, when it is most vulnerable.**

Now, let's talk about something very practical—**cash flows**. Your expenses are predictable, but markets are not. If your entire portfolio is invested in volatile assets, you may be forced to sell at the wrong time—when markets are down. That can permanently damage your portfolio.

A simple solution is to create a buffer. Set aside 2–3 years of expenses in relatively stable instruments. For example, if your annual expense is ₹6 lakhs, set aside ₹12–18 lakhs in low-volatility assets.

This ensures that your regular expenses are not dependent on market conditions and gives your long-term investments time to recover.

Your fourth investment goal is to align your portfolio with your **cashflow needs so that withdrawals do not disrupt your plan.**

Finally, there is the most underestimated factor—**your own behaviour**. A well-designed plan often fails not because it was wrong, but because it was not followed. Markets will test you. There will be periods when returns look disappointing, your portfolio underperforms expectations, and negative news dominates the environment.

In such times, the biggest risk is not the market; it is how you react to it. If your portfolio makes you anxious enough to abandon it, then it is the wrong portfolio, regardless of how it looks on paper.

Your final investment goal is simple, but critical: **build a portfolio that you can stick with.**

So, your investment goals in retirement are not just about chasing returns. They are about getting a few critical things right: earning returns that beat inflation after withdrawals, managing drawdowns you can live through, protecting against poor return sequences, aligning investments with your cashflow needs, and ensuring you stay invested through market cycles.

Get this right, and everything else—including product selection becomes significantly easier.

19

The Ideal Asset Allocation for Retirement

Let me tell you about two retirees, both 65 years old, both with approximately ₹2 crore corpus, both needing roughly ₹10 lakhs annually to fund their retirement gap.

The first had put everything in fixed deposits. "Safe and steady," he said. "I can't afford to lose money at my age." His FDs were earning 6.5%, generating ₹13 lakhs annually. After 30% tax, that became ₹9.1 lakhs. His expenses were ₹10 lakhs. He was short ₹90,000 in the very first year. With inflation at 6%, his expenses next year would be ₹10.6 lakhs, while his post-tax FD income would remain at ₹9.1 lakhs. He was eating into principal from year one, and the gap widened every year.

The second retiree had done the opposite. Ninety per cent of his corpus was in equity—small-cap mutual funds, mid-cap stocks, sectoral bets. "I need growth to beat inflation," he explained. Then 2020 happened. His portfolio dropped 45% in two months from ₹2 crores to ₹1.1 crores. He needed ₹10 lakhs for annual expenses, but withdrawing from a portfolio that had just halved meant selling at devastating losses. He panicked, sold half his equity at the bottom, and moved it to FDs. The market recovered, but his portfolio didn't because he'd locked in losses by selling low.

Two retirees. Two extreme strategies. Both failing in different ways. One's excessive safety guaranteed slow erosion from inflation. The other's excessive aggression guaranteed panic during volatility. Neither had built a portfolio that could sustain 30 years of retirement.

This chapter is about the middle path—the asset allocation that balances safety with growth, that survives market crashes without panic-selling, that beats inflation without taking reckless risks.

WHY EXTREMES ALWAYS FAIL IN RETIREMENT

The asset allocation that worked during your accumulation years won't work during retirement. When you were 35 and earning a salary, you could afford to be 80% in equity because you had 25 years until retirement and a monthly income to fall back on if markets crashed. When you're 65 and withdrawing from corpus, that same allocation is financial suicide. But 100% debt is equally dangerous, just slower and less obvious.

Here's why all-debt fails. You retire with ₹2 crores in fixed deposits earning 6.5%—₹13 lakhs annually. Year one, you need ₹10 lakhs. You're fine. Year five, inflation-adjusted expenses are ₹13.5 lakhs. Your FD income is still ₹13 lakhs. Now you're eating principal. Year ten, you need ₹18 lakhs. Your corpus has shrunk to ₹1.6 crores from principal withdrawals. FD income is down to ₹10.4 lakhs. The gap widens every year. By year 20, you're desperate. By year 25, you're out of money, with potentially another 10 years to live. Safety killed you—slowly, quietly, but just as surely as a market crash.

Here's why all-equity fails. You retire with ₹2 crores, 90% in equity. Markets do well initially. Year three, a major crash—markets drop 50%. Your portfolio is now ₹1.15 crores. You need ₹11 lakhs for expenses. Withdrawing ₹11 lakhs from ₹1.15 crores is a 9.6% withdrawal rate—unsustainable. You're forced to sell equity at the worst possible time, locking in permanent losses. Even if markets recover over the next three years, your portfolio won't because you kept selling through the downturn. You're in a death spiral, shrinking corpus, forced selling during downturns, never fully participating in recoveries. Volatility killed you—quickly, painfully, irreversibly.

Neither extreme works. You need both debt and equity in the right proportions, for the right reasons, managed with discipline.

THE THREE ROLES ASSETS PLAY IN RETIREMENT

Different assets serve different purposes in your retirement portfolio.

Debt is your stability layer. It funds your near-term expenses, sits calmly through market crashes, and lets you sleep at night knowing your next 2–3 years of expenses are secure, regardless of equity markets. Debt doesn't make you rich. It keeps you safe.

Equity is your growth engine. It beats inflation over long periods, rebuilds your corpus even as you withdraw, and ensures your purchasing power doesn't erode over 30 years. Equity is volatile and terrifying during crashes, but essential for long-term survival. Without equity, inflation slowly destroys you.

Gold is your crisis hedge. It typically moves differently from both debt and equity, sometimes up when both are down, sometimes sideways. Gold doesn't generate income or grow dramatically. But it's insurance against catastrophic scenarios—currency collapse, extreme inflation, geopolitical chaos. You hope you never need it. You're glad it's there anyway.

Real estate is complicated. Your primary residence isn't part of your investment portfolio; it's shelter. Investment property generating rental income is predictable income, not portfolio allocation. Vacant land or property you're "holding for appreciation" is speculative and probably not appropriate for retirement portfolios that need liquidity and income.

Your job is to combine these assets in proportions that give you enough stability to survive crashes, enough growth to beat inflation, and enough flexibility to adjust as markets and needs change.

THE FOUR NON-NEGOTIABLE RULES

Any retirement portfolio must follow these rules. These are not suggestions, but requirements.

RULE 1: MINIMUM 10% IN EACH MAJOR ASSET CLASS

Your portfolio must have at least 10% in debt, at least 10% in equity, and at least 10% in gold. Real estate doesn't count towards this rule because a single property can represent 30%–50% of total assets and would skew everything. Your liquid portfolio—debt, equity, gold must follow the 10% rule.

RULE 2: DEBT MUST FUND AT LEAST THREE YEARS OF EXPENSES

This is the most important rule for portfolio survival. Your debt allocation should fund three full years of annual expenses without touching equity or gold.

Why three years? That's longer than most market downturns last. The 2008 crisis took about 30 months from peak to recovery. The 2020 COVID crash recovered faster, but uncertainty lasted longer. Three years gives you the buffer to never sell equity at a loss during crashes.

If you need ₹10 lakhs annually, your debt allocation should be at least ₹30 lakhs. Make it ₹35–40 lakhs to account for inflation during those three years. This money sits in fixed deposits, liquid funds, ultra-short-term debt funds—boring, safe, immediately accessible.

When markets crash, you don't panic. You don't sell equity at losses. You calmly withdraw from your debt buffer and wait for recovery. Once markets recover and equity rebuilds, you rebalance—sell some of your equity gains and replenish your debt buffer to three years' worth.

If you can afford it, make it five years of expenses in debt instead of three. That's even safer. But three years is the absolute minimum.

Below that, you're forced to sell equity during downturns, which destroys retirement portfolios permanently.

RULE 3: NO CONCENTRATION - EVER

Within each asset class, you must diversify properly.

In equity: no single stock should exceed 10% of your equity allocation. No single sector should exceed 25%. Individual stocks fail catastrophically. If you're 30 with a salary, you can afford concentrated bets. If you're 65 and retired, you cannot. One bad stock destroying 25% of your portfolio could mean the difference between a sustainable retirement and running out of money.

In debt: no single corporate bond or debt instrument should exceed 10% of your debt allocation—except government bonds, which are safe and can be higher. The more risk an instrument carries, the less of it you should own. Government bonds? 50%–60% of debt allocation is fine. AAA-rated corporate bonds? 10%–15% each maximum. Anything below an AA rating? Not appropriate for retirement portfolios at all.

RULE 4: MATCH ALLOCATION TO YOUR REALITY, NOT GENERIC ADVICE

Every adviser gives age-based formulas: "100 minus your age in equity." That gives a 65-year-old 35% equity. Reasonable starting point, but not customised to your actual situation.

Your allocation depends on your withdrawal rate (higher rate needs more equity), your health (poor health needs more liquid debt), your family support (if you have family support, you can increase equity allocations), your risk tolerance (if 30% drops cause panic, reduce equity regardless of formulas), and your alternative income (pension or rental income reduces pressure on corpus and allows more equity).

A 65-year-old with 3% withdrawal rate, excellent health, and pension income can handle 45% equity comfortably. A 65-year-old with 6% withdrawal rate, diabetes, and no other income should probably be at 40% equity maximum. Know yourself. Know your situation. Adjust accordingly.

HOW DO YOU KNOW WHAT IS THE BEST ALLOCATION FOR YOU?

Here is a simple 5-step process to identify the best allocation for you.

Step 1: Start with a minimum allocation of 10% across all asset classes.

Step 2: Define the target rate of return that you seek on your overall portfolio. If you are targeting higher returns, you will need to allocate a higher amount to equity.

Step 3: Do a Drawdown Analysis to know your risk tolerance. Would you still be comfortable with the equity allocations you decided in Step 2 if the market dropped by more than 50% tomorrow? If yes, you can stick to your targeted allocation. Else, you will have to reduce the allocation.

Step 4: Ensure that no asset class ever goes beyond 60%. A higher allocation to equity, debt, gold, or real estate suggests that you continue to carry your investment biases.

Step 5: Ensure that you have liquidity that can fund 3–5 years of expenses. If not, reduce equity exposures to meet this requirement.

THE ANNUAL REBALANCING RITUAL

Markets move, your allocation drifts, and suddenly you're no longer following your plan.

You start at 55% debt, 35% equity, 10% gold. Equity rallies 25%. Debt grows 7%. Gold drops 5%.

By year-end, without you doing anything, you're at 48% debt, 40% equity, 9% gold—more aggressive than intended, more exposed to volatility than planned.

Or equity crashes 30%, and suddenly you're 65% debt, 23% equity, 10% gold—far more conservative than intended, meaning you'll underperform inflation going forward.

This is allocation drift. It happens automatically and destroys portfolios if uncorrected.

The solution is systematic annual rebalancing. Once a year, pick a specific date and make it a ritual to review your portfolio and rebalance it back to target allocations.

If equity has outperformed and grown beyond the target, sell enough to bring it back down to the target. Use those proceeds to buy more debt or whatever has underperformed. You're systematically selling high and buying low. If equity has crashed below target, sell some debt (which stayed stable) and buy more equity while it's down. Again, buying low systematically.

This feels wrong emotionally. When equity is soaring, selling feels like missing out. When equity is crashing, buying feels like catching a falling knife. But this counter-emotional discipline is what makes portfolios work over decades.

Without rebalancing, you drift towards whatever performed best recently, exactly when it's most dangerous. With rebalancing, you systematically move money away from what's expensive towards what's cheap. Over 20–30 years, this makes an enormous difference.

Rebalance annually. Not monthly (too much transaction cost). Not "whenever I feel like it" (you won't). Pick your birthday, pick January 1st, pick Diwali. Make it a ritual that happens every single year without fail.

Your Turn: Review the targeted asset allocation part in Section 5 of your Retirement Plan.

You have the rules, the recommendations, and the rationale. Now make actual decisions about your specific portfolio.

THE ALLOCATION THAT LETS YOU SLEEP

The best asset allocation isn't the one that maximises returns on a spreadsheet. It's the one that lets you sleep at night, doesn't make you panic-sell during crashes, and gives you the confidence to stick with the plan for decades.

If 40% equity makes you check your portfolio obsessively and lose sleep during every 10% correction, drop to 30% equity. The slightly lower returns are worth the significantly higher peace of mind. Portfolios don't fail due to suboptimal allocations; they fail due to panic selling and abandoning the plan.

Eventually, both retirees I mentioned earlier learned this. After watching his corpus erode from all-debt, the first reluctantly moved to 60% debt, 30% equity, 10% gold. "I'm nervous about the equity," he admitted. "But I'm more nervous about running out of money at 80."

After his painful 2020 experience, the second restructuring was to 55% debt, 35% equity, 10% gold. "I sleep better now," he said. "And I'll never be forced to sell at the bottom again."

Both after failing with extremes found the middle path. Not exciting. Not optimal. But sustainable. That's what retirement portfolios need to be: sustainable for 30 years. Everything else is secondary.

Build yours accordingly.

CHECKLIST: THE IDEAL ASSET ALLOCATION FOR RETIREMENT

1. Do you have a complete list of all your investments? (Yes/No)
2. Do all asset classes have at least 10%–15% allocated to them? (Yes/No)
3. Are your investment return expectations realistic and not anchored to the past? (Yes/No)
4. Will the investment returns that you expect from your portfolio exceed the expected rate of inflation after accounting for your expenses? (Yes/No)
5. Are you comfortable with the expected drawdown of your overall portfolio? (Yes/No)
6. Are you aware of the taxation aspects of all the investments in your portfolio? (Yes/No)
7. Can you fund your expenses for 3–5 years even if the stock market were to shut down? (Yes/No)
8. There is no single investment (except government bonds) that is more than 10% of your investment portfolio. (Yes/No)
9. Can you access at least 80% of your investment portfolio within 5 days? (Yes/No)
10. There is no product in the investment portfolio that you do not understand. (Yes/No)

If all the answers are "Yes" to all the questions, you have arrived at an ideal asset allocation for Retirement.

20

The Stress Test

You've built your Desi Retirement Plan. You've calculated your expenses, set aside money for your promises, built your healthcare defence, determined your income gap, assessed your corpus, calculated your withdrawal rate, and allocated your assets across debt, equity, gold, and real estate.

On paper, everything looks perfect. Your withdrawal rate is 3.8%, comfortably within the gold-standard zone. Your asset allocation is balanced. Your plan should work for 35 years.

But here's the uncomfortable truth: your plan is only as good as your assumptions. And every assumption you've made—about expenses, about healthcare costs, about inflation, about investment returns—could be wrong.

Not slightly wrong. Dramatically wrong.

This chapter is about stress-testing your plan by deliberately breaking your assumptions to see what happens when reality doesn't follow your spreadsheet. Because it won't. It never does.

WHY ASSUMPTIONS ALWAYS BREAK

Let me tell you what happened to someone who thought his plan was bulletproof.

He retired at 60 with ₹3 crores, needing ₹12 lakhs annually—a comfortable 4% withdrawal rate. He'd calculated everything carefully. His expenses were based on three years of actual spending data. His healthcare buffer was ₹25 lakhs. His asset allocation was textbook-perfect: 55% debt, 35% equity, 10% gold. He'd even stress-tested a 10% increase in expenses and remained comfortable.

In year 3 of retirement, his wife was diagnosed with a rare neurological condition. The treatment wasn't covered by insurance: experimental therapy, not yet approved. Cost: ₹18 lakhs over two years. His healthcare buffer was depleted by year 5.

In year 6, his daughter got married. He'd budgeted ₹30 lakhs. But gold prices had doubled since he'd made that estimate, and family expectations had grown. Actual cost: ₹48 lakhs.

In year 8, his son lost his job during a recession and needed support for 18 months. ₹12 lakhs he hadn't planned for.

By year 10, his ₹3 crore corpus was down to ₹1.8 crores, not from market losses, but from expenses he'd underestimated or never imagined. His withdrawal rate had jumped from 4% to 6.7%. At 70 years old, with potentially 25 more years to live, he was in crisis.

He had followed the rules. But his assumptions had broken—not one assumption, multiple assumptions, all in the same decade. And broken assumptions compound. One underestimated expense depletes the corpus, increasing the withdrawal rate and making every subsequent expense more damaging.

This is why stress-testing matters. Not to scare you. To prepare you.

STRESS TEST #1: YOUR EXPENSES ARE 20% HIGHER THAN YOU THINK

Your first stress test is simple and brutal: assume your actual retirement expenses will be 20% higher than you've calculated.

Not because you're bad at math. But because you're human, and humans consistently underestimate their future needs. You forget things. You undercount irregular expenses. You assume discipline you won't maintain. You don't account for lifestyle creep. You calculate "minimum comfortable" and forget that "comfortable" costs more in practice than in theory.

Here's how to run this test. Take your annual expenses—let's say ₹15 lakhs. Increase by 20%: ₹18 lakhs. Now recalculate your withdrawal rate with this higher number.

If your corpus is ₹4 crores and your original withdrawal rate was 3.75% (₹15 lakhs ÷ ₹4 crores), your stress-tested withdrawal rate becomes 4.5% (₹18 lakhs ÷ ₹4 crores).

You went from comfortably within the gold-standard zone to the upper edge of safety. Still manageable, but much less margin for error.

Now try the test with your own numbers:

If your stress-tested withdrawal rate stays below 5%, you're fine. You have a cushion. Even if you've underestimated expenses, you're still in safe territory.

If your stress-tested rate goes to 5%–6%, you're now in the caution zone. You don't have much buffer. You need to either cut expenses somewhere or accept that you're walking a tighter line than you thought.

If your stress-tested rate exceeds 6%, you're in danger territory even without anything going wrong. This is your wake-up call. Go back to your expense calculations. Find the padding. Where did you underestimate? Monthly lifestyle expenses? Family obligations? Social and cultural costs? Healthcare premiums? Be brutally honest. Because if a 20% increase in expenses breaks your plan, your plan was already fragile.

STRESS TEST #2: MEDICAL EMERGENCIES COST 100% HIGHER THAN YOUR ESTIMATES

The second stress test is even more uncomfortable: assume you had a medical emergency that cost 100% higher than planned.

Why 100% instead of 20%? Because healthcare is the category where underestimation is most severe and most common. People in good health convince themselves they'll stay healthy. People who've never dealt with serious illness can't imagine what it costs. People budget for "normal" medical expenses and never account for the catastrophic ones.

Here's the test.

You've set aside ₹30 lakhs for the healthcare defence fund.

Increase by 100%: ₹60 lakhs needed.

That extra ₹30 lakhs must come from somewhere. It comes from your retirement corpus. If your retirement corpus was ₹3 crores, your actual retirement corpus is now ₹2.70 crores. If you were funding an annual expense of ₹15 Lakh, your AWR was a comfortable 5%. The stress-tested AWR is now 5.55% (₹15L ÷ ₹2.7 crores).

You just jumped from the gold standard to the danger zone purely due to a freak healthcare expense.

This test is especially critical for people currently in excellent health. If you're 58, exercise regularly, have no chronic conditions, and feel invincible, you're most likely to under-budget healthcare. You won't feel invincible at 75. Budget accordingly now.

STRESS TEST #3: INFLATION RUNS HIGHER THAN EXPECTED

Your third stress test addresses the assumption that might break most dramatically: inflation.

You've probably planned assuming 5%–6% inflation. That's the long-term average. It's reasonable. It's also not guaranteed.

India has experienced periods of 10%–12% inflation. We've had years of 3%–4% inflation. Globally, we've seen countries experience hyperinflation (Argentina, Venezuela, Zimbabwe, where inflation exceeded 100% or even 1000% annually) and prolonged deflation (Japan, where prices fell for decades).

You can't specifically plan for these extremes—hyperinflation makes all planning meaningless, and deflation changes the entire economic structure. But you can understand what happens if inflation runs consistently higher than your assumption for a decade or more.

Let's say you've planned for 6% inflation, but actual inflation runs at 8% for your first 15 years of retirement. Your expenses, which you expected to grow from ₹15 lakhs today to ₹36 lakhs in year 15 (at 6% inflation), grow to ₹47.5 lakhs (at 8% inflation). That's 32% higher than you planned.

Meanwhile, your investment returns are linked to inflation. If inflation is higher, nominal returns increase somewhat but not proportionally. Debt that was returning 7.5% in a 6% inflation environment might return 9% in an 8% inflation environment (real return drops from 1.5% to 1%). Equity that was returning 12% might return 10% (real return drops from 6% to 2%).

Your expenses increased 32% more than planned. Your returns increased only modestly. Your corpus depletes faster than your spreadsheet predicted.

You can't perfectly stress test for this because there are too many variables. But you can do a simplified test: assume your effective inflation rate is 1.5 percentage points higher than planned, and your returns increase by only 1 percentage point.

In practice, this means if you planned for 6% inflation and 9% portfolio returns (3% real return), stress test for 7.5% inflation and

10% portfolio returns (2.5% real return). Your real purchasing power erodes 0.5 percentage points faster per year. Over 20 years, that 0.5% compounds, you end up with roughly 10%–12% less purchasing power than planned.

The answer to this stress test isn't to panic. You can't perfectly predict inflation. But you can be aware that your margin for error is smaller than you think if inflation runs hot.

What to do if this concerns you: Build in slightly more conservative assumptions. Plan for 6.5% inflation instead of 5.5%. Lower your expected real returns by half a percentage point. Accept a slightly higher withdrawal rate in your base plan, so you have a cushion if inflation surprises you.

WHAT STRESS-TESTING ACTUALLY REVEALS

Here's what these three stress tests tell you: they reveal how fragile or robust your plan is.

If all three stress tests leave you still in the gold-standard zone (below a 5% withdrawal rate, even after adding 20% expenses, 50% higher healthcare, and slightly higher inflation), your plan is robust. You can absorb significant surprises and still be fine. Congratulations—you've built genuine security.

If one stress test pushes you into the 5%–6% range but the others keep you below 5%, your plan is moderately robust. You can handle some surprises, but not multiple surprises simultaneously. Be vigilant. Monitor expenses closely. Don't inflate lifestyle. Be ready to adjust if needed.

If two or more stress tests push you above 5%, or if any single test pushes you above 6%, your plan is fragile. It works only if your assumptions hold. But assumptions rarely hold perfectly. You need to make changes before retiring—work longer, save more, reduce planned expenses, increase predictable income, something.

And if all three stress tests push you significantly above 6%, your plan isn't a plan—it's a hope. Don't retire yet. The probability of running out of money is too high.

THE TWO SCENARIOS YOU CAN'T REALLY PLAN FOR

Stress-testing has limits. There are two extreme scenarios where traditional planning breaks down entirely: deflation and hyperinflation.

Deflation—sustained falling prices—sounds good, but is economically devastating. When prices fall year after year, people defer purchases (why buy today when it'll be cheaper tomorrow?), businesses can't raise prices or wages, unemployment rises, and investments lose value. Japan experienced this for two decades. In a deflationary environment, holding cash seems smart, but investment returns collapse. Debt instruments lose value as issuers default. Even "safe" strategies fail.

Hyperinflation—prices rising 100% or 1000% annually—destroys currency-based planning entirely. If a loaf of bread costs ₹100 today and ₹1,000 next month, your retirement corpus denominated in rupees becomes meaningless. Argentina, Venezuela, and Zimbabwe—all experienced this. In hyperinflation, only hard assets (gold, real estate, foreign currency) retain value.

You can't meaningfully plan for either scenario. If they occur, everyone's plans break, not just yours. The financial system restructures. What you can do: maintain reasonable diversification (including gold, which tends to hold value in extremes), don't have all assets in one currency if you can help it, and understand that in a true crisis, adaptability matters more than planning.

But don't obsess over these extremes. They're low-probability events. Focus your stress-testing on realistic variations—expenses 20% higher, healthcare 50% more, inflation 1–2 percentage points off—because these are likely, not theoretical.

THE EMOTIONAL STRESS TEST: CAN YOU ACTUALLY STICK TO THE PLAN?

There's one more stress test that's not about numbers.

It's about you.

When markets crash 40%, can you stick to your asset allocation and rebalance by buying more equity? Or will you panic and sell?

When your neighbour buys a new car and takes a luxury vacation, and you're cutting discretionary expenses because your withdrawal rate is 5.2%, can you stay disciplined? Or will you give in to lifestyle creep?

When your son needs help with a business investment, and you've already funded his wedding and his education, can you say no? Or will you deplete your corpus further because saying no feels cruel?

When you're 72 and healthcare costs are higher than planned, and your corpus is smaller than hoped, can you cut expenses where needed? Or will you maintain your lifestyle until you run out of money?

This emotional stress test is harder than the numerical ones. Because numbers are logical. Emotions aren't.

The only way to pass this test is honest self-assessment. Are you disciplined under pressure? Can you make difficult choices? Can you live with less if needed? If you're not sure, build even more cushion into your plan. Because plans don't fail due to bad math; they fail due to human behaviour.

LIVING THROUGH THE CRISIS: WHAT NOT TO DO

Finally, let's talk about what happens when you're in retirement, and something breaks—markets crash, inflation spikes, medical crisis hits, or all three simultaneously.

You will face these moments. Not once. Multiple times over 30–40 years. How you respond determines whether your plan survives.

Here's what not to do, because these actions destroy more retirement plans than any market crash:

Don't abandon your asset allocation in panic. When equity markets drop 40%, your instinct will be to sell everything and move to "safety." Don't. You'll lock in losses at the worst possible time. Remember why you have three years of expenses in debt, so you never have to sell equity during crashes. Use your debt buffer. Wait for recovery. It will come. It always has.

Don't chase returns during bubbles. When everyone around you is making 30% returns in crypto, small-cap stocks, or real estate, your instinct will be to join. Don't. You're not trying to get rich anymore. You're trying not to get poor. Chasing returns means taking risks you can't afford. Stick to your allocation. Boring wins in retirement.

Don't inflate lifestyle during good years. When markets rally, and your corpus grows, your instinct will be to increase spending, take bigger vacations, give more gifts to family, and make lifestyle upgrades. Don't, or at least, be very careful. Good years should rebuild your buffer, not justify higher permanent expenses. Because bad years will come, and you'll wish you'd saved that cushion.

Don't ignore warning signs. If you're three years into retirement and you've already had to dip into your healthcare buffer, increase your withdrawal rate to 6% and delay rebalancing because you can't bring yourself to sell equity, these are red flags. Don't ignore them. Adjust now while you still can—cut expenses, generate income, something. Small course corrections early prevent disasters later.

What should you do instead? Stick to your plan. Maintain asset allocation. Rebalance annually even when it feels wrong. Use your debt buffer during crashes. Cut discretionary expenses temporarily during crises. Keep perspective—every market crisis in history has eventually been resolved. This one will too.

Your emotions will scream at you to do something. Usually, the right answer is to do nothing except follow the plan you built when you were thinking clearly.

A FINAL THOUGHT ON STRESS-TESTING

Stress-testing isn't about creating anxiety. It's about creating preparedness.

The person who does the stress tests and discovers fragility has time to fix it—work longer, save more, adjust expectations. The person who doesn't stress test discovers fragility at age 72 when options are limited, and panic is high.

You've spent this entire book building your Desi Retirement Plan. You've done the work. You've been thoughtful. Now make sure your plan can survive contact with reality.

Because the goal isn't to have a perfect plan that works if everything goes right. The goal is to have a robust plan that survives when things go wrong.

And things will go wrong. They always do. The question is whether you'll be ready.

Don't ignore stress test results. They're not theoretical. They're showing you what happens when life doesn't follow your spreadsheet. And life never follows spreadsheets.

With this, we conclude our discussions on how to think and build an investment portfolio that works well in your retirement years. In the next section, we will discuss investment products that are relevant from a retirement perspective.

PART - IV

THE DESI INVESTMENT PRODUCTS

21

The SLRT Framework for Smarter Investment Choices

In this section, we will explore the investment options that work best in your retirement years, focusing not just on what to invest in but also on how to choose wisely.

Retirement investing is less about chasing the highest returns and more about creating a balance between stability, accessibility, growth, and tax efficiency.

To make this process simpler and more structured, we begin with a guiding framework: the SLRT Framework, which stands for Safety, Liquidity, Returns, and Taxation. This framework will serve as a practical lens for evaluating any investment product and understanding the trade-offs involved.

Building on this foundation, the next chapter (Chapter 22) looks at investments that generate predictable and regular income—helping you meet your essential expenses with confidence.

The following chapter (Chapter 23) then expands the lens to growth-oriented and tax-efficient income options, which introduce some variability but play a crucial role in helping your portfolio stay ahead of inflation over time.

Together, these three chapters aim to give you both clarity and confidence in constructing a retirement portfolio that is stable, sustainable, and adaptable.

HOW TO EVALUATE EVERY INVESTMENT BEFORE YOU INVEST?

Before you talk about any investment, it is important to pause for a moment. The real problem in retirement investing is not the lack of options. In fact, if anything, there are too many options available today. The real problem is the lack of clarity on how to choose between them.

Most people invest based on what sounds good, what someone recommends, or what seems to be working at that point in time. Very rarely do they have a clear and structured way to evaluate what they are investing in. And that is where things begin to go wrong. Over time, this leads to a portfolio that looks reasonable on the surface but is poorly aligned with real-life needs.

What you need is not more products. You need a simple way to judge every product before you put your money into it. A framework that forces you to think clearly and completely.

This is where the SLRT Framework comes in. It stands for Safety, Liquidity, Returns, and Taxation.

These are the four questions you must ask before investing in anything. Not just once, but every single time you make an investment decision.

To understand why this matters, consider a far more common situation.

A retired couple had parked a large part of their savings—around ₹50 lakhs into a real estate investment. It was a second property in a developing suburb. The logic seemed sound. "Property always goes up," they were told. "It's a solid, long-term asset." There was no immediate need for the money, so locking it into real estate felt comfortable.

A few years later, circumstances changed. Their son wanted support for a business opportunity. They needed to arrange funds within a few months. They decided to sell the property.

That's when reality hit.

There were no buyers at the expected price. The market had slowed down. Every serious inquiry came with a steep discount. Brokers advised them to lower expectations if they wanted a quick sale. What looked like a ₹50 lakh asset on paper could fetch only ₹40–42 lakh in a time-bound sale.

They had wealth, but they did not have access to it.

Eventually, they had to arrange funds through other means at a cost while the property remained unsold.

Nothing was fundamentally wrong with real estate as an asset. But the investment had never been evaluated fully.

They had focused on one belief, "property appreciates," and ignored the more important questions. This is exactly where the SLRT Framework helps. It forces you to step back and ask the right questions before you commit.

S FOR SAFETY

Can I lose my money? Before anything else, you need to understand the safety of your investment. This begins with a few simple but critical questions:

1. Can I lose my principal?
2. If yes, will the loss be temporary or permanent?
3. What is the worst-case scenario?
4. Can I afford that outcome?

Safety is not just about whether an investment can fall in value. Almost every investment, at some point, will. The real question is whether that loss is something you can recover from.

Instruments like fixed deposits and government-backed schemes offer a high degree of safety. Your capital is largely protected. On the other hand, equity markets can fluctuate sharply. Real estate can stagnate or decline depending on location and timing. Corporate bonds carry the risk of default.

But an equally important distinction is between temporary and permanent loss. A fall in equity markets may reduce your portfolio value for a period, but it can recover if you stay invested. A defaulted bond or a failed investment, however, may result in a permanent loss of capital.

In retirement, this distinction becomes critical. Temporary declines can be managed if you have the time and the liquidity to wait. Permanent losses, however, reduce your financial base in a way that cannot be repaired. That is why the objective is not to eliminate risk, but to avoid irreversible mistakes. Diversification plays a key role here. It ensures that no single event can significantly damage your portfolio.

L FOR LIQUIDITY

Can I access my money when I need it? The next dimension is liquidity, and it is often underestimated until it is needed. Ask yourself:

1. How quickly can I convert this investment into cash?
2. What will it cost me to exit?
3. Will I get fair value if I need to sell quickly?
4. Can I afford to keep this money locked for years?

Liquidity is not just about whether you can sell an investment. It is about whether you can sell it when required, at a reasonable price, without significant loss.

Bank deposits and liquid funds offer near-instant access. Equity mutual funds and listed stocks can be liquidated within a few days. But assets like real estate or certain bonds can take months to sell, especially if market conditions are not favourable.

The cost of liquidity is equally important. Breaking a fixed deposit may involve a small penalty. Selling a property quickly may require a large discount. In such cases, the investment may have value, but it does not provide flexibility.

A retirement portfolio must always include assets that are easily accessible. Because financial security is not just about how much you have, it is also about how quickly you can use it when needed.

R FOR RETURNS

Will my money grow meaningfully? Returns are the most visible part of any investment, but they are also the most misunderstood. Before getting carried away by numbers, ask:

1. What is the expected return?
2. How does it compare with inflation?
3. What will I earn after taxes?
4. How stable or volatile are these returns?

A return figure, by itself, tells you very little. What matters is how that return affects your purchasing power.

If your investment earns 7% and inflation is 6%, your real growth is minimal. On the other hand, an investment earning 11% to 12% over time may create meaningful wealth, but it may also come with periods of sharp decline along the way.

This is where behaviour becomes important. A volatile investment may offer higher long-term returns, but only if you are able to stay invested through difficult phases. If you exit during downturns, the actual return you experience may be far lower.

Returns, therefore, must always be evaluated in context, after inflation, after taxes, and along with the journey you will need to endure.

T FOR TAXATION

How much of my return will I keep? The final dimension is taxation. It is often ignored, but it has a direct and lasting impact on your outcomes. Ask yourself:

1. How is this investment taxed?
2. What is my post-tax return?
3. Are there more tax-efficient alternatives?
4. Am I using available exemptions effectively?

Two investments with similar returns can deliver very different outcomes after tax. Interest income from deposits is fully taxable. Equity investments may benefit from a lower long-term capital gains tax rate. Certain instruments offer tax advantages that can improve overall returns.

In retirement, when income is more structured and often limited, tax efficiency becomes even more important. The return that matters is not what you earn—it is what you keep.

Ignoring taxation may not seem significant in the short term, but over time, it can meaningfully reduce the effectiveness of your portfolio.

BEYOND SLRT: ONE MORE DIMENSION TO CONSIDER

The SLRT Framework covers the fundamentals. But let me add one more dimension that matters a lot, specifically for retirement portfolios: **Complexity.**

Can you understand this product completely? If someone asks you to explain how it works, can you do it clearly in two minutes?

If not, don't invest in it. Retirement portfolios should be simple enough that you can manage them at age 75, or that your spouse can manage them if you're incapacitated, or that your children can understand them if they need to help.

Complex structured products, derivatives, exotic investments—these have no place in retirement portfolios. Not because they're always bad, but because the complexity hides risk you won't see until it's too late.

When you look at investments through the lens of Safety, Liquidity, Returns, Taxation, and Complexity, a simple truth emerges. Every investment is a trade-off. There is no perfect product that excels on all five dimensions. Some offer safety but lower returns. Others offer higher returns but come with volatility. Some are tax-efficient but less liquid.

Your role is not to find perfection. Your role is to create balance.

The SLRT Framework helps you do exactly that. It forces you to evaluate investments completely, rather than partially. Over time, this discipline protects you from attractive-looking but unsuitable products, from decisions driven by emotion, and from mistakes that are difficult to reverse.

Before you invest in anything, pause and ask yourself these simple questions. Is it safe enough for your needs? Is it liquid enough for your situation? Are the returns realistic when seen in the right context? And how much of those returns will you keep after tax? Can you explain the product easily?

If you cannot answer these questions clearly, it is better to wait than to proceed with uncertainty.

In retirement, investing is not about chasing the best opportunity; it is about avoiding the wrong ones.

A simple framework, applied consistently, will do far more for your financial security than any complex strategy.

In the chapters that follow, we will apply this framework to different investment options, so that you can make decisions with clarity and confidence.

22

Investment Products for Generating Predictable Income

At the heart of every retirement portfolio lies one non-negotiable requirement: the certainty that your essential expenses will be met, month after month, without you having to worry. This chapter is about the investment products designed to deliver exactly that. They are not built to maximise growth. They are built to minimise uncertainty, and in retirement, that is often the more important objective.

The four categories covered here are Bank Fixed Deposits, Government Bonds, Tax-Free and Taxable Bonds, and Annuities. Each has its own vocabulary, its own mechanics, and its own trade-offs. Understanding them well is not just an academic exercise. These instruments, chosen thoughtfully and combined intelligently, can form the income layer of a retirement portfolio that never keeps you awake at night.

Before we go product by product, a word on how to read the ratings at the end of each section. Each dimension—Safety, Liquidity, Returns, Taxation, and Complexity—is scored on a scale of 1 to 5. The scores are the author's personal assessment and do not constitute investment advice. No product scores 5 across all dimensions, and that is precisely the point. Retirement planning is not about finding the perfect product. It is about intelligently combining imperfect ones. Here is what each of the scores means.

Score	What it means
Safety	
1	Speculation • high chance of significant capital loss
2	High risk• Potential to lose significant amount of capital
3	Moderate risk • potential to lose some capital
4	Low risk • capital largely protected
5	Zero risk to capital loss
Liquidity	
1	No liquidity, capital is fully locked in
2	Liquid but only with significant discounts
3	Liquid with moderate discounts
4	Liquid, access funds within 3 to 5 days
5	Highly liquid, access funds within a day at **full** market value
Returns	
1	Low returns, do not beat inflation
2	Returns generally match inflation
3	Moderate returns, beat inflation by 1% to 2%
4	High returns, potential to beat inflation by 3% to 6%
5	Significant returns, potential to beat inflation by 6% or more
Taxation	
1	No taxation benefit
2	Some taxation benefit
3	Moderate tax benefits
4	Highly tax efficient
5	Tax free
Complexity	
1	Very simple, universally understood
2	Simple, low risk, predictable returns
3	Moderate, need to interpret market terminology
4	Complex, requires credit research or financial analysis
5	Very Complex, requires advanced knowledge and strategies

1. BANK FIXED DEPOSITS

The comfort of certainty

For many retirees, fixed deposits are not just an investment; they are a habit. They offer something deeply reassuring—you know your return, you know your tenure, and you know your bank will give your money back. There is no need to track markets, no decisions to make mid-stream, and no fear of volatility. That simplicity is powerful. But it also comes with a quiet cost that compounds over time.

Fixed deposits are available for tenures ranging from seven days to 10 years. When used to generate regular income, the challenge is what investment managers call reinvestment risk. Most investors naturally gravitate towards the tenure offering the highest interest rate, often one to three years. When that deposit matures and rates have fallen, the income from the next deposit is lower. You had no say in that. The market decided for you.

Over time, inflation further erodes the purchasing power of returns, and taxation—interest from FDs is added to your income and taxed at your slab rate, quietly takes another bite. What feels completely safe today can become quietly insufficient over a retirement that lasts 20 or 30 years. Fixed deposits work well as a starting point. They rarely work well as a complete solution.

SLRT Score: Bank Deposits

Safety	Liquidity	Returns	Taxation	Complexity
4–5	3	2	1	1

Simplest product to invest in. Post-tax, post-inflation returns are thin. Safe bank selection matters.

2. GOVERNMENT BONDS (GILTS AND SDLS)

The safest investment you can make.

If fixed deposits are about comfort, government bonds are about safety. When you invest in a government bond, you are lending money to the government in exchange for a fixed stream of income. In return, the government promises to pay you a fixed interest rate, called a coupon, every six months, and to return your original investment, called the face value, when the bond matures. Think of it as giving the government a loan.

Since the government issues these bonds, the credit risk—the risk that your principal does not come back is effectively zero. That certainty makes government bonds the natural backbone of a retirement income portfolio.

THE TWO TYPES YOU NEED TO KNOW

Central government securities, commonly called Gilts, are bonds issued by the Government of India through the Reserve Bank of India. The name comes from British times, when these certificates literally had gold-edged, gilt-edged borders, symbolising their rock-solid guarantee. Gilts are issued for tenures ranging from five to 40 years. For a retiree, that 40-year option is remarkable; it means you can lock in an interest rate for virtually your entire retirement, knowing both the income and the principal return are guaranteed.

State Development Loans, or SDLs, are bonds issued by individual state governments—Maharashtra, Gujarat, Tamil Nadu, and others to fund their development programmes. They are typically issued for five to 10 years and pay interest every six months. Because state governments are considered marginally less secure than the central government, SDLs pay a slightly higher interest rate. The additional return is modest but real, and many retirees hold a mix of Gilts and SDLs to capture it.

THE LANGUAGE OF BONDS

Government bonds have their own vocabulary, and getting comfortable with it is worth the effort.

The face value—sometimes called par value is the original price of the bond, usually ₹100 per unit, and it is what you receive back at maturity.

The coupon rate is the annual interest rate: a bond with a 7% coupon on a face value of ₹100 pays ₹7 per year, or ₹3.50 every six months.

The yield is the actual return you will earn, which can differ from the coupon if you buy the bond at a price other than face value—buy at ₹95 and your yield is higher than 7%, because you are getting the same ₹7 on a smaller investment. The maturity date is when the government returns your principal.

When buying or selling bonds in the secondary market, you will encounter two prices. The clean price is the bond's quoted price, without any accumulated interest. The dirty price, also called the settlement price, is what you pay, including the interest that has built up since the last coupon payment was made.

When you buy a bond midway through an interest period, you compensate the seller for the interest they have earned up to that point. When you sell, the buyer compensates you. Once you understand this, the arithmetic becomes straightforward.

THE ONE RISK THAT MATTERS

Government bonds are traded in the secondary market every day, and as interest rates change, so do bond prices, always in the opposite direction. When rates rise, existing bond prices fall. When rates fall, bond prices rise. The sensitivity to this movement increases with the remaining life of the bond: a bond with three years left will fall far less when rates rise than one with 10 years remaining. The worked example is worth holding in your mind. Suppose you buy a 10-year bond at ₹100 paying 7% interest. A year later, new bonds are being issued at 8%. Your 7% bond now looks less attractive, and its market price falls to perhaps ₹95. If you sell, you lose ₹5. But if you do not sell, the loss is only on paper. Hold until maturity, and you will receive all your interest payments and your full ₹100 back. The price risk only crystallises if you sell before maturity.

There are two straightforward ways to manage this. The first is simply to hold bonds until maturity. The second is to ladder your holdings by buying bonds of different tenures simultaneously, say 5, 10, 15, and 20 years. When rates rise, the shorter-maturity bonds will have fallen far less in price. If you need to sell before maturity, you sell those first. Laddering also means you always have bonds maturing at regular intervals, giving you both liquidity and the opportunity to reinvest at prevailing rates.

HOW TO BUY GOVERNMENT BONDS

The RBI Retail Direct platform allows individual investors to participate directly in weekly government bond auctions, without going through a broker. The auction process requires some familiarisation, but the RBI website explains it clearly, and the effort is worth making—you buy at the same price as institutional investors, with no intermediary fee. Alternatively, if you have a demat account, bond trading platforms such as NSE goBID allow you to browse available bonds by tenure, yield, or issuer and place orders directly. A sensible approach for first-time bond investors is to begin with a small amount, ₹10,000 to ₹20,000, to understand the mechanics before committing larger sums.

SLRT Scores: Government Bonds

Safety	Liquidity	Returns	Taxation	Complexity
5	3	3	1	3

Zero credit risk. Returns improve with longer tenures. Requires comfort with bond market vocabulary.

3. TAX-FREE AND TAXABLE BONDS

When the issuer matters as much as the return.

Beyond government bonds, a wide range of bonds are issued by public sector undertakings, government-backed institutions, and private corporations. Tax-free bonds are typically offered by PSUs and government agencies, and entities like NHAI, REC, PFC, and IRFC, while taxable bonds are issued by both public and private sector companies. The distinction matters because interest from tax-free bonds is exempt from income tax, which makes them disproportionately attractive to investors in higher tax brackets. A taxable bond yielding 8% and a tax-free bond yielding 6% deliver the same after-tax return to someone in the 30% bracket, but the tax-free bond does it with considerably less administrative complexity.

Tax-free bonds typically have long maturities, often 10 to 20 years, making them well-suited for retirement portfolios where predictable income over an extended period is the goal. Taxable bonds offer more varied tenures and generally higher nominal yields, but the net return depends heavily on your tax situation. Both types can be purchased in the primary market— through public issues that work much like an IPO—or subsequently in the secondary market through a broker or trading platform. Liquidity in the secondary market is moderate; these bonds do trade, but not as actively as equities, and a patient investor who holds to maturity will find them straightforward.

UNDERSTANDING CREDIT RATINGS

Because taxable bonds are issued by entities whose creditworthiness varies, understanding credit ratings is essential before investing. Rating agencies—CRISIL, ICRA, and CARE in India, and Standard & Poor's, Moody's, and Fitch internationally—assess each issuer's ability to repay interest and principal on time and express that assessment as a letter rating. A suffix of + or − refines the grade: AA+ is stronger than AA, which is stronger than AA−.

Rating	What it means
AAA to AA	Highest quality, very safe. The issuer's ability to repay is not in doubt.
BBB to A	Moderate quality, some risk present, but still investment grade.
BB and below	Speculative, higher risk of default, higher potential return.
D	Default, the issuer has already failed to meet its obligations.

For retirement portfolios, the practical guidance is to stay within investment-grade bonds and resist the temptation of higher-yielding, lower-rated instruments. The additional return rarely compensates for the additional risk when you are dependent on that income. Among investment-grade options, the trade-off is straightforward: higher-rated bonds offer more safety; lower-rated ones within the investment-grade range offer slightly more income.

SLRT Scores: Tax-Free and Taxable Bonds

Safety	Liquidity	Returns	Taxation	Complexity
3–5	3	3	2–5	3

Safety depends on credit rating. Tax-free bonds are highly efficient for investors in the 30% bracket.

4. ANNUITIES:

An answer to the question no one wants to ask

At the heart of retirement lies a question most people would rather not confront: what if I live longer than my money? Annuities exist precisely to answer it. You pay a lump sum called the purchase price to an insurance company, and in return, the company pays you a guaranteed income for the rest of your life. However long you live, the payments continue. The longevity risk, which is the risk of outliving your corpus, transfers entirely from you to the insurer.

Annuities are the structural opposite of life insurance. With life insurance, you pay regular premiums, and your family receives money when you die. With an annuity, you pay once, and the company pays you for as long as you survive. Think of it as creating your own pension from scratch. The vocabulary is distinct from other financial products and worth knowing precisely, because the choices you make at purchase cannot easily be undone.

THE VOCABULARY YOU NEED

The amount you invest is the purchase price, not a premium. The regular income you receive is called the annuity or pension. You are the annuitant. The annuity rate tells you how much annual income you will receive per lakh invested: if the rate is 6%, a purchase price of ₹10 lakhs generates ₹60,000 per year. A life annuity pays for as long as you live. A joint life annuity continues paying your spouse after your death. And the return-of-purchase-price option means your original investment is returned to your nominee when you die, in exchange for a lower annuity during your lifetime.

HOW THE NUMBERS WORK

The table below shows illustrative annual annuity amounts paid by Life Insurance Corporation of India on a purchase price of ₹1 lakh. These rates are linked to prevailing market interest rates and will vary over time—treat these figures as indicative rather than definitive.

Your Age	With return of purchase price (₹)	Without return of purchase price (₹)
50	6,520	7,710

Your Age	With return of purchase price (₹)	Without return of purchase price (₹)
60	6,600	8,930
70	6,730	11,650

Two things stand out in those numbers. First, opting to forgo the return of purchase price materially increases your annuity; at age 70, the difference is nearly ₹5,000 per lakh per year. Second, the older you are when you buy, the higher your annuity, which is the reverse of life insurance, where younger buyers pay less. The insurer is pricing your longevity: a 70-year-old has a statistically shorter remaining life, so the company can afford to pay more per year. A practical implication follows: buying an annuity when interest rates are high locks in higher rates for life. If rates in the economy are low, it is worth waiting.

TWO SCHEMES WORTH KNOWING

The Pradhan Mantri Vaya Vandana Yojana is a government-subsidised annuity scheme available exclusively to those aged 60 and above, managed by LIC. It offers an assured return of 7.4% per annum as of 2025, though this is reviewed annually on a purchase price of up to ₹15 lakhs per person over a 10-year policy period. The full purchase price is returned either at the end of 10 years or on death, whichever comes first. A loan facility is available after three years, and surrenders are permitted in cases of critical illness. The scheme has been extended several times; verify its availability and current rates before planning around it.

Saral Pension, introduced by the insurance regulator IRDAI in 2022, is a standardised immediate annuity product that every life insurance company is required to offer with identical features. Available to anyone between 40 and 80 years of age, it offers a choice between single and joint life options, with the purchase price returned to nominees on the death of the last annuitant. Because the features are identical across all insurers, the only variable that matters when choosing a provider is the annuity rate. Rates can differ by 0.25%–0.50% across companies, modest in percentage terms, but meaningful when compounded over a lifetime of payments.

THE HONEST TRADE-OFFS

Annuities offer something genuinely rare in financial products: the guarantee of income for life, regardless of how long that life turns out to be. For covering essential expenses—rent, food, utilities, medications—this guarantee has real value. The disadvantages are equally real. The annuity rate is fixed at purchase, so a fixed income that seemed adequate at 60 may feel pinched at 80 after two decades of inflation. The money is largely illiquid; once committed, it cannot easily be redirected. And the returns, while guaranteed, are modest on a post-tax basis; they may barely keep pace with inflation. Annuities work best not as the entirety of a retirement income strategy but as its floor: the layer that ensures the non-negotiables are always covered, no matter what else happens.

SLRT Score: Annuities

Safety	Liquidity	Returns	Taxation	Complexity
4–5	1	2	1	3

Guaranteed lifetime income. Low liquidity by design. Tax inefficient for higher bracket investors. Many product variants.

No single product in this chapter does everything. Fixed deposits offer simplicity but modest real returns. Government bonds offer safety and long-term certainty but require comfort with bond mechanics. Tax-Free Bonds are effective for tax-sensitive investors but are illiquid. Annuities eliminate longevity risk but lock away your capital. The skill in retirement income planning is not in finding the one right product—it is in combining these instruments so that each covers the gaps the others leave.

The next chapter turns to the other side of the retirement portfolio—the investments that do not offer predictable income but can grow your corpus and keep pace with inflation over the long term. Both layers are necessary. This one gives you the floor. The next chapter helps you build above it.

23

Investment Products for Growth-Oriented Income and Tax Efficiency

While predictable income provides stability, retirement can span decades, which makes it equally important to ensure your income keeps pace with rising costs. Inflation, even at moderate levels, steadily erodes purchasing power over time. What comfortably covers your expenses today may fall noticeably short 10 or 15 years down the line. This is where growth-oriented income plays a vital role. Investments such as mutual funds, REITs, and InvITs offer the potential for income that can grow over time, helping you stay ahead of inflation rather than merely keep pace with it.

Fixed-income products are dependable, but their returns are largely static. Over long periods, inflation can outstrip those returns, gradually reducing your real income—the amount you receive stays the same, but what it can buy keeps shrinking. Growth-oriented investments address this gap by introducing the possibility of increasing income and capital appreciation, albeit with some variability along the way. Used thoughtfully alongside stable income sources, they help create a more resilient retirement strategy, one that not only preserves your financial security but also protects your lifestyle over the long term.

1. MUTUAL FUNDS

A mutual fund is a simple idea with powerful consequences. It collects money from many investors and puts that pooled capital to work across a mix of assets—bonds, shares, or a combination of both. Each investor owns units in the fund, and the value of those units changes daily as the underlying investments perform. In other words, a mutual fund lets your money be managed by professionals, with full transparency and flexibility, at a fraction of the cost of private wealth management.

The benefits are well established. Professional managers decide where to invest, so you do not need to track markets daily. Even a modest investment is spread across many companies and bonds, which reduces concentration risk. Most funds can be redeemed within one to three business days. Investments and valuations are disclosed daily. You can begin with as little as ₹500. And the tax treatment of mutual funds, particularly for long-term investors, can be significantly more efficient than that of bank fixed deposits or bonds paying periodic interest.

For the purposes of generating growth-oriented income in retirement, three broad fund families are relevant: Debt Funds, Hybrid Funds, and Equity Funds. Each sits at a different point on the risk-return spectrum and serves a different role in a retirement portfolio.

DEBT FUNDS - THE CALM, STEADY SAILORS

Debt funds invest exclusively in fixed-income instruments—government securities, corporate bonds, bank certificates of deposit, and money market instruments.

They have no exposure to equities and are consequently far less volatile than equity markets.

For retirees, debt funds can serve as a flexible and professionally managed alternative to fixed deposits. They offer similar predictability of income, but with the added advantages of daily liquidity, the possibility of capital appreciation when interest rates fall, and in many cases, greater tax efficiency on gains held for longer periods.

The category is broad. Liquid and money market funds are suited to parking short-term cash. Short-duration funds work well for a one to three-year horizon. Corporate bond funds invest in high-quality company debt and offer slightly higher yields than pure government funds. Gilt funds, which invest only in government securities, carry no credit risk. Dynamic bond funds actively adjust their portfolio in response to changing interest rate expectations. Each variant suits a different need, and a well-constructed retirement income strategy may use more than one.

HYBRID FUNDS - THE MIDDLE PATH

Hybrid funds invest across asset classes, typically a mix of equity and debt, sometimes with an allocation to gold or other assets, and it is this blend that makes them particularly well-suited to retirement portfolios. By combining growth-oriented assets with stabilising ones, hybrid funds aim to reduce volatility relative to pure equity funds while generating returns meaningfully above those of pure debt funds.

If the ideal retirement investment were to be described—decent returns, reasonable tax efficiency, daily liquidity, automatic rebalancing, and minimal need for active monitoring—hybrid funds come closer to that description than almost anything else available to individual investors.

Balanced Advantage Funds, or BAFs, are among the most useful in this category. They function like automatic gears in a car: the fund manager adjusts equity exposure dynamically based on a model-driven view of market valuations. When equity markets are expensive, the fund reduces equity and moves into debt. When markets are cheap, it increases equity. This happens automatically, without any intervention from the investor. Because BAFs maintain equity exposure above 65%, including through arbitrage strategies that reduce market risk while keeping the equity allocation high, they qualify for equity-style taxation, which is meaningfully more favourable than debt fund taxation for most investors.

Multi-Asset Funds invest across three or more asset classes—typically equity, debt, and gold, sometimes extending to real estate or international equities. The diversification this creates is not merely mathematical. When one asset class underperforms, another may compensate, keeping overall returns steadier. Gold tends to perform well when equities struggle, providing a natural buffer. Multi-Asset Funds offer genuine diversification, inflation protection through both equity and gold, and generally lower volatility than pure equity funds, making them a practical choice for investors who want broad exposure without managing multiple separate positions.

EQUITY FUNDS - GROWTH OVER THE LONG TERM

Equity funds invest primarily in shares of companies across market capitalisations, sectors, and geographies, depending on the fund's mandate. They exhibit the highest volatility among the three fund families, but also the greatest potential for long-term capital appreciation. For retirees, this might seem counterintuitive. Why hold an asset class that can fall 30%–50% in a bad year? The answer lies in two facts. First, retirements now routinely span 25 to 30 years, which means a portion of the portfolio still has a genuinely long investment horizon. Second, over any rolling ten-year period in Indian market history, equity has outperformed every other major asset class, including gold, real estate, and fixed deposits. Abandoning equity entirely at retirement means forfeiting returns that are difficult to replicate elsewhere.

The practical approach for retirees is not to hold equity funds as a primary income source, but as a growth engine for the portion of the corpus that will not be drawn upon for at least 7 to 10 years. Large-cap funds, which invest in the hundred largest companies by market capitalisation, offer the most stability within the equity category. Flexi-cap and diversified multi-cap funds spread risk across company sizes. Index funds and ETFs, which simply replicate a market index like the Nifty 50 or Sensex, provide equity exposure at the lowest possible cost with no active management risk. For most retirees, a modest allocation to a well-diversified equity fund, alongside debt and hybrid holdings, is not a risk to be managed but a return to be earned.

FIXED DEPOSITS VS SYSTEMATIC WITHDRAWAL PLANS

The mechanism for drawing regular income from mutual funds is the Systematic Withdrawal Plan, or SWP. It works as the mirror image of the more familiar SIP. In an SIP, you invest a fixed amount periodically and accumulate units over time. In an SWP, you instruct the fund to redeem a fixed amount periodically—monthly, quarterly, or annually; the proceeds are credited to your bank account. The fund calculates how many units need to be redeemed to meet each payment and does so automatically.

Let us compare an investment in a bank FD with an SWP in a mutual fund. In case of a bank FD, you are paid interest on a quarterly basis. If the FD rate was 6% p.a., you got paid 1.5% every quarter. With your investment of ₹10 lakh in a bank FD, which earns an interest of 6% p.a., it would pay you ₹15,000 as interest on a quarterly basis, as banks generally pay interest quarterly.

If the same investment of ₹10 lakh was done in a mutual fund (like a debt fund or hybrid fund), you set up a SWP by instructing the mutual fund to withdraw the amount you wish to withdraw and the periodicity of the payment. If you instructed the MF to pay you on a quarterly basis at a similar bank FD rate, you would request a SWP of ₹15,000 per month. The mutual fund would redeem units equivalent to this amount from your investments and pay out this amount to you every quarter. In case the fund returns were higher than what you have requested, the same would remain a part of your investments, and in case there was a shortfall, you would see some reduction in your originally invested amount.

The table below illustrates this with a worked example. An investment of ₹10 lakhs is made in January 2025. A quarterly SWP of ₹15,000 is set up. The fund generates a return of 7% during 2025.

Date	Trx. Type	Transaction Value (Rs.)	NAV	Units allotted or redeemed	Unit Balance	Cap. Gains	Value of initial investment
1-Jan-2025	Pur.	+10,00,000	200.0	5000.0	5000.0	NA	10,00,000
1-Apr-2025	SWP	-15,000	204.0	73.5	4926.4	294	10,04,985
1-Jul-2025	SWP	-15,000	210.0	71.4	4855.0	714	10,19,550
1-Sep-2025	SWP	-15,000	216.1	69.4	4785.6	1110	10,34,168
1-Jan-2026	SWP	-15,000	214.0	70.1	4715.5	982	10,09,117

** The fund generated a return of 7% in 2025.*

The value of your investments would be ₹10,09,117 on 1 January 2026 after withdrawals of ₹60,000 during the year.

The beauty is that part of your withdrawal comes from returns, and part from the capital—but it's all seamless, tax-efficient, and managed by the fund house.

The biggest advantage of SWP is tax efficiency. Though your total withdrawals were ₹60,000, the capital gains amount is just ₹3,100. This feature of SWP makes SWP very attractive for investors in the highest tax brackets. Please note that the taxable amount would increase with the passage of time as the difference between the Buy NAV and Sell NAV increases. But the good news is that it will be relatively lower for a similar investment in fixed deposits.

SLRT Score: Mutual Funds

Safety	Liquidity	Returns	Taxation	Complexity
2–4	3–4	2–4	2–4	3

Risk depends on fund type—lowest for debt, higher for equity. SWP is highly tax-efficient for regular income.

2. REITS AND INVITS

Real estate and infrastructure - without the headaches

Real Estate Investment Trusts own and manage income-producing commercial properties. When you buy units of a REIT, you own a fractional interest in a portfolio of high-value properties—office buildings, shopping malls, warehouses, hotels, data centres—managed by a professional team. The income you receive comes from the rents those properties generate.

Infrastructure Investment Trusts, or InvITs, work on the same principle but invest in infrastructure assets instead: highways and toll roads, power transmission lines, renewable energy projects, gas pipelines, and telecom towers. The economics are similar—stable, long-term cash flows from assets that require significant capital to build but generate income reliably once operational.

These structures solved a fundamental problem that had long kept individual investors out of commercial real estate and infrastructure: the capital requirement. To own a premium office building directly, you needed crores. Through a REIT, you can own a proportional interest in multiple premium properties across India for ₹10,000. You also avoid the practical burdens of direct ownership—tenant disputes, maintenance, property management, vacancy periods—which are handled by professional managers. REITs are required to distribute at least 90% of their income to unit holders, which means you receive the rental cash flows directly and regularly. Units trade on the stock exchange, so your investment is liquid in a way that direct property never is.

HOW REITS AND INVITS GENERATE RETURNS

You make money in two ways. The first is regular distributions—rental income from properties in the case of REITs, and toll or transmission revenues in the case of InvITs, paid quarterly or half-yearly.

The key driver of income is occupancy: well-managed REITs maintain occupancy above 90%, translating into predictable and growing rental income.

For InvITs, the income driver is usage: traffic on toll roads, power demand on transmission lines, and, in many cases, the concession agreements allow for tariff escalation over time, meaning income can grow. The second source of return is capital appreciation: as property values and infrastructure asset values increase, so does the NAV of your investment.

For retirees, the inflation-protection dimension of these assets is particularly relevant. Commercial rents are typically reviewed and periodically reset upward. Toll collections grow as traffic increases. The distributions you receive today are likely to be higher five or 10 years from now than they are at the time of investment, unlike the coupon from a fixed-rate bond, which remains unchanged throughout its life. This combination of regular income and inflation-linked growth is precisely what a retirement portfolio needs.

THE VOCABULARY YOU NEED

The Net Asset Value, or NAV, is the actual value of all properties or infrastructure assets in the trust divided by the number of units outstanding. If the NAV is ₹400 but the unit trades at ₹450 on the exchange, you are paying a premium to the underlying asset value. The Distribution Per Unit, or DPU, is the cash paid out to you per unit in each distribution cycle. If the DPU is ₹8 per quarter and you hold

100 units, you receive ₹800 every quarter. The yield is the annual DPU divided by the unit price—a unit trading at ₹400 with an annual DPU of ₹32 carries an 8% yield. For InvITs, the concession period is the length of time the trust has the contractual right to operate the infrastructure and collect revenues. A highway InvIT might have a 20-year concession to collect tolls on a particular stretch.

WHAT TO WATCH OUT FOR

The risks in REITs and InvITs are real and worth understanding before investing. Unit prices fluctuate daily based on market sentiment, even when the underlying assets are performing steadily—a REIT holding fully occupied prime offices can still see its unit price fall 15% if interest rates rise, because rising rates make the fixed distributions from the REIT comparatively less attractive. This interest rate sensitivity is structurally similar to that of bonds and is managed in the same way: by holding for the long term rather than responding to short-term price movements. Economic slowdowns can affect occupancy rates and toll traffic, temporarily reducing distributions.

Some REITs and InvITs are concentrated in a single geography or asset type, which amplifies the impact of any sector-specific problem. A diversified portfolio of two or three REITs and InvITs is preferable to a large position in any single one.

REITs and InvITs are bought and sold on the stock exchange in the same way as shares. You need a demat account. India launched its first REIT, Embassy Office Parks REIT, in 2019, and several others have followed. There are also publicly listed InvITs focused on highways and power transmission. The NSE website and the Indian REITs Association provide useful research resources. A sensible starting point is ₹25,000 to ₹50,000 spread across two or three different trusts, with a focus on those with diversified underlying portfolios rather than single-asset concentration.

SLRT Scores: REIT and InvIT

Safety	Liquidity	Returns	Taxation	Complexity
3	3–4	2–3	2–3	3

Moderate risk linked to real estate or infrastructure. Component-based distribution taxation requires some familiarity.

BRINGING IT ALL TOGETHER

Retirement investing is not about finding a single perfect product. It is about combining different types of investments, so they complement each other, each covering what the others cannot.

The products discussed across this chapter and the previous one—fixed deposits, government bonds, tax-free bonds, annuities, debt and hybrid equity funds, REITs, and InvITs—each have genuine strengths and genuine limitations. None is sufficient on its own. Together, used in the right proportions, they create something none of them can create alone: a portfolio that is simultaneously safe enough, liquid enough, tax-efficient enough, and growing fast enough to sustain a retirement that may last three decades.

The SLRT Framework has given you a consistent lens through which to evaluate any investment, not just the ones in these two chapters, but any product you encounter in the future. By assessing Safety, Liquidity, Returns, Taxation, and Complexity together rather than optimising for any one of them, you make decisions that are grounded in your actual needs rather than in whichever dimension is being marketed most aggressively at any given moment.

Predictable income products form the foundation: they cover essential expenses and provide the stability that allows you to sleep at night. Growth-oriented investments add a layer of resilience that keeps your portfolio viable throughout your retirement, not just the first decade. Neither is sufficient alone. Together, they create the balance that a well-constructed retirement portfolio requires.

Your income needs, risk tolerance, and market conditions will all change over time. The portfolio you build today should be designed to evolve, reviewed periodically, rebalanced deliberately, and adjusted as your life changes. With the right framework and a balanced mix of products, you can move forward knowing that your money is working not just to support your present but to protect your future.

The next section of the book focuses on how you can maximise your desi retirement years—the decisions and habits that make a difference between a good retirement and a great one.

PART - V

MAXIMISING YOUR RETIREMENT YEARS

24

Passing on Your Legacy

Chapter 24 will help you strengthen Section 6: Passing on your Legacy of your Desi Retirement Plan.

I am sure all of you are aware of the thousands of crores sitting unclaimed in Indian banks, insurance companies, mutual funds, and provident fund accounts right now. Money that belongs to someone or belonged to someone who passed away without telling anyone it existed.

These are life savings, pension payments, insurance payouts, and investment redemptions gathering digital dust in financial institutions across India, waiting for someone to claim them. Except nobody knows they exist.

According to recent RBI data, unclaimed deposits in banks have been growing at an alarming pace. Insurance regulator IRDAI reports that thousands of crores in life insurance claims go unclaimed because families don't even know policies exist. SEBI estimates that over ₹20,000 crores in shares and mutual funds remain unclaimed.

These aren't abandoned fortunes from people who had no family. These are normal middle-class Indians who worked hard, saved diligently, built wealth carefully, and then died without telling anyone where their money was.

The bitter irony: They secured their families financially, then made it impossible for their families to access that security.

You've spent this entire book building your Desi Retirement Plan. You've calculated your expenses, planned for healthcare, optimised your investments, and worked towards a sustainable withdrawal rate. Now you have a corpus—₹1.5 crores, ₹3 crores, ₹5 crores—that will support you through retirement and likely leave something behind for your children or causes you care about.

But here's the uncomfortable question: When you're gone, will your family be able to access that money? Or will it join the crores trapped in bureaucratic limbo?

You would not wish that your wealth goes to the wrong people, gets stuck in legal disputes, or simply disappears because nobody knew it existed. This chapter is about making sure that doesn't happen.

WHY NOBODY DOES THIS (UNTIL IT'S TOO LATE)

If legacy planning is so important, why do so few people do it? Here are the real reasons—not the excuses they give, but the truth underneath.

The most common reason is simple denial. Death feels distant, theoretical, something that happens to other people. You're 62, healthy, and active. Why worry about wills and nominations now? You'll get to it... eventually. Then one day, it's not eventual anymore. And your family discovers you never got around to it.

Indian culture doesn't encourage talking about death. Planning for your own death feels like inviting bad luck, like you're somehow manifesting your demise by preparing for it. So, people avoid the conversation entirely. They don't make wills. They don't update nominations. They don't tell anyone where their investments are. Because talking about these things feels uncomfortable.

Many parents assume their children are smart enough to find everything. "They know I have mutual funds. They know I have insurance. They'll contact the companies and sort it out." Except they won't because they don't know which companies, which account numbers, which branch, which adviser. And without that information, "figuring it out" takes years.

Then there's the trust dilemma. If you write down all your account numbers, passwords, and assets, what stops someone from stealing from you while you're alive? If you share everything with your son, what if he runs into financial problems and gets tempted? If you share with your daughter-in-law, what if there are tensions in the marriage? So, you share nothing. And when you die, nobody can access anything.

Finally, the paperwork feels overwhelming. Making a will requires lawyers. Updating nominations requires visiting multiple offices. Creating an inventory requires digging through years of documents. It's easier to postpone. Until one day, it's too late.

These reasons are understandable. But they're also dangerous. Because the cost of not planning isn't borne by you, it's borne by your family.

WHEN LEGACY PLANNING FAILS

Let me tell you what happens when someone dies without proper legacy planning.

Raghavan Uncle was 68 when he died suddenly of a heart attack. He'd been healthy and active, planning to travel more. His death shocked everyone. His son Arvind flew in from Dubai. His daughter Priya came from Bangalore. Both assumed settling their father's affairs would take a few weeks—signing some papers, closing some accounts, distributing the assets.

Three years later, they're still not done.

They knew Raghavan Uncle had money. Good amount. He'd been a successful accountant, saved diligently, invested carefully. The house was paid off. There was a corpus—they just didn't know how much or where. Which banks? Which mutual fund companies? Which demat accounts? Which insurance policies? Which FDs? Nothing was written down. There was no will. Most nominations hadn't been updated in 20 years—some still listed Raghavan's father, who'd died 15 years ago.

In the first three months, they searched the house. Found old bank passbooks, some mutual fund statements from 2015, a few insurance papers, and random fixed deposit receipts. No comprehensive list. So, they wrote to every bank and financial institution they could think of. "Did our father have an account with you?" Most replied after 60 days. Some never replied at all.

By the end of the first year, they'd discovered multiple accounts—HDFC, ICICI, SBI, three different PSU banks, and two cooperative banks. Each required separate paperwork. Death certificates. Legal heir certificates. Succession certificates in some cases.

The second year, the real problems emerged. One mutual fund account had ₹25 lakhs but no nomination. Required succession certificate from the court—a 9-month process. One life insurance policy worth ₹18 lakhs had already been claimed... by someone who'd forged documents. Legal battle ensued.

Year three, they're still fighting. One bank claimed no account existed until they found a dormant account with ₹8 lakhs that hadn't been touched in 15 years. Another mutual fund house said the units were transferred to IEPF because dividends went unclaimed for 7 years. Getting that money back? Another legal process.

Meanwhile, Arvind had to fly to India four times from Dubai—visa costs, flight tickets, hotel stays, time away from work. Priya burned through her leave days and had to take unpaid leave. Legal fees exceeded ₹3 lakhs. The emotional toll? Incalculable.

All because Raghavan Uncle never spent three hours creating a proper legacy plan.

This isn't unusual. This is typical.

THE THREE PILLARS OF LEGACY PLANNING

Legacy planning doesn't have to be complicated. You don't need expensive lawyers for everything. You don't need to create elaborate trust structures. You need three things done properly: a complete asset map showing every rupee you own, an access bridge so your family can find and claim everything, and a legal shield protecting it all through proper documentation.

Let's build each pillar, starting with the simplest one.

PILLAR ONE: THE COMPLETE ASSET MAP

The foundation of legacy planning is brutally simple: write everything down. Not just major investments. Everything. Because what seems insignificant to you, that ₹2 lakh FD from 2018, is impossible for your family to find if you don't document it.

Start with bank accounts. List every bank, every branch, every account number, every type of account—savings, current, fixed deposits. Write down approximate balances and who's nominated. Then move to investments. Write down every mutual fund folio, which AMC, distributor, or platform; every demat account, which depository participant. List your direct equity holdings, bonds, and government securities, your PF and pension accounts with EPF numbers and NPS PRAN. Insurance policies with policy numbers and companies.

Don't forget physical assets. Properties with addresses, registration details, and current market value. Gold and jewellery—approximate weight, location, locker details if applicable. Vehicles with registration numbers. And increasingly important these days, digital assets. Internet banking credentials. Email accounts that receive financial statements. Cryptocurrency wallets, if you have any.

List your liabilities too. Outstanding loans, guarantees given to others, and money owed to or from family members. And finally, important contacts: write the name, phone number, and email of your financial adviser, your chartered accountant, insurance agent, lawyer, bank relationship manager, and demat account manager.

You have three options for creating this map. The simple spreadsheet—create an Excel file with separate tabs for each category, update it every six months, and print it out annually. The physical ledger—some people prefer writing by hand in a dedicated notebook because it feels more secure, not being digital. Or the digital vault using services like password managers or Google Drive with proper security.

Choose the method that you will maintain. A perfectly organised system you never update is useless. A simple notebook you update religiously is gold.

Mark one day each year—your birthday, New Year's Day, whatever as your asset map update day. Go through every account, update balances, add new investments, remove closed accounts, verify contact details, and check nominations. This takes two to three hours once a year. That's it. That's the entire maintenance requirement.

PILLAR TWO: THE ACCESS BRIDGE

You've created the asset map. Now comes the harder question: How do you give your family access to this information without making yourself vulnerable while you're alive? This is the trust dilemma. The information that helps your family after your death could potentially be misused while you're alive.

The solution is to create two separate documents. The first document, call it your Emergency Access File, contains just enough information for someone to find your assets if you die suddenly, without giving them the ability to access those assets while you're alive. It lists all banks by name and branch, all mutual fund companies and platforms, insurance companies, demat account providers, property addresses, the location of original documents, and the contact numbers of your financial adviser, CA, and lawyer. Notice what it doesn't include—no account numbers, no passwords, no PINs, no specific balances.

Why this works is elegant. If you die, your family knows which institutions to contact. They'll say, "Our father passed away. Did he have an account with you? Here's the death certificate." The institution will verify and share details. Your family can access everything legally. But while you're alive, this document doesn't give anyone the ability to access your accounts or steal from you.

The second document, your Complete Details File, contains everything—account numbers, passwords, current balances, and specific instructions. Store this in a bank locker or home safe that only you can access while you're alive. In your will, specify that upon your death, specific people are authorised to access this locker or safe.

Beyond documents, you need a trusted guardian. This is one person—spouse, adult child, sibling, or trusted adviser who knows your financial landscape. They know Document 1 exists and where to find it. They receive an annual update conversation from you about major changes. They don't have access to accounts or passwords while you're alive. They're named in your will as the person authorised to access Document 2.

Choose this person carefully. They must be younger than you, financially literate enough to understand what you're telling them. They must be trustworthy, but don't need access to everything today. And ideally, they're not someone with financial troubles that might tempt misuse.

Once a year, sit with this person for 30 to 60 minutes. Tell them about major changes. You're not sharing account numbers or passwords. You're just making sure someone knows the landscape.

But what if you genuinely don't trust anyone completely? Maybe family relationships are strained. Maybe you're a single person with no close relatives. Maybe you've been betrayed before and can't bring yourself to trust again. You have options.

Your lawyer or chartered accountant can be named as executor of your will. They're bound by professional ethics. They won't access anything while you're alive, but upon your death, they're legally authorised to execute your wishes. This typically costs ₹25,000–₹50,000 to set up, plus a percentage of the estate value upon execution.

Or use a partial sharing strategy. Your son knows about mutual funds. Your daughter knows about bank accounts. Your brother knows about property. No single person has complete access, but collectively, they can reconstruct everything. This isn't perfect; if these people don't communicate well, it creates confusion. But if total trust in one person isn't possible, distributed information might be your best option.

PILLAR THREE: THE LEGAL SHIELD

Now we come to legal documentation—nominations, wills, and the processes that ensure your wishes are executed.

Start with nominations. They're not legally binding inheritance—they're administrative convenience. When you nominate someone on a bank account or mutual fund, you're saying: "Upon my death, give this money to this person quickly, without waiting for legal processes." Without a nomination, your mutual fund worth ₹25 lakhs requires a succession certificate from the court before the AMC will release money. This takes six to 12 months minimum. With a nomination, your nominee presents a death certificate, fills out a claim form, and receives money within 30 to 45 days.

You need nominations on every bank account, every mutual fund folio, every insurance policy, every demat account, EPF and NPS accounts, and bank lockers. Most can be updated online now. Log in to your account, look for the update nomination option, fill the form, and submit. Some require physical forms sent by post.

The critical mistake people make is outdated nominations. I've seen policies where the nominee is someone who died 10 years ago. Or someone from whom you're now estranged. Review and update every three to five years. And yes, you can nominate multiple people. Specify 50% to son, 50% to daughter. Or 100% to spouse with children as contingent nominees if spouse predeceases you.

Now, the Will. A Will is a legal document that specifies exactly who gets what after you die. Unlike nominations, which are just administrative, a Will is legally binding. You need to understand some basic vocabulary first.

You are the testator—the person making the will. The executor is the person you appoint to execute your will. They'll handle the paperwork, distribute assets, and ensure your wishes are followed. Choose someone younger than you, financially competent, and trustworthy. The beneficiaries are the people who inherit—your spouse, children, siblings, charities, whoever you want. If you have minor children, you must name a guardian who'll take care of them, which is different from the executor who handles money.

Probate is the legal process of validating your will in court. Required for some assets like property in major cities, not required for others like bank accounts with nominations. A succession certificate is a court document that proves who your legal heirs are and is required when there's no Will or nomination.

Your Will must include clear identification of yourself, revocation of all previous wills, an executor appointment, distribution of specific assets, a residuary clause catching everything you forgot to list, and your signature witnessed by two people who are not beneficiaries.

You can get a will drafted by a lawyer for ₹10,000 to 25,000. The advantage is that it's professionally done, legally sound, and the lawyer can store a copy. The disadvantage is that it costs money and requires appointments. Alternatively, you can use template wills that are free or cheap, though they might miss legal nuances. My recommendation:

for estates above ₹50 lakhs or complex family situations—second marriages, estranged relatives, specific wishes—use a lawyer. For simple estates, a well-drafted template can work.

You can register your will at the sub-registrar's office for a nominal fee. This creates an official record that the will exists, prevents claims it was forged or destroyed, and makes it easier for your executor to prove the will is genuine. The downside is that it becomes part of the public record and is slightly more cumbersome to change. My take: register it. The advantages outweigh the disadvantages for most people.

Update your will every five years and after major life events—marriage, divorce, birth of children or grandchildren, death of beneficiaries, major changes in assets, or relationship changes like becoming estranged from someone you'd named as executor.

Let me briefly walk you through what your family will face even with perfect planning. They'll need multiple original death certificates—get 10 to 15 issued immediately. For some claims, especially property and large amounts, they'll need a legal heir certificate from the SDM or tehsildar. Then, for each financial institution, they submit a death certificate, a legal heir or succession certificate if there is no nomination, fill out claim forms, provide account details, and wait 30 to 90 days for processing.

Your family doesn't pay inheritance tax—India doesn't have one currently. But they inherit your tax liabilities, any pending income tax returns you should have filed, and capital gains on assets when they eventually sell those assets.

One critical thing: if you have physical share certificates, bonds, or debentures, get them dematerialised immediately. Physical certificates are a nightmare for heirs. Companies won't recognise them easily. Transfers take months or years. Some companies have shut down their physical transfer offices entirely. Open a demat account if you don't have one. Contact your broker with the physical certificates, fill in the dematerialisation request form, submit the certificates, and within 15 to 30 days, the shares will appear in demat form. Do this now, not someday, because if you die with physical certificates, your family needs succession certificates, will probate, and 12 to 18 months to even start the transfer process.

Your Turn: Review Section 6: Passing on your Legacy of your Desi Retirement Plan

It does not end here.

THE PERIODIC LEGACY PLANNING RITUAL

Here's your simple process. Every year, or once every three years on the same date, spend a total of four hours. First hour, update your asset map—review all accounts, add new investments, remove closed accounts, update balances. Second hour, check nominations—log in to accounts, verify nominations are current, update if family situation has changed. Third hour, review your will—read it and ask if anything major has changed; visit a lawyer to update if yes. Fourth hour, have your guardian conversation—brief update on changes this year; ensure they know where documents are.

Four hours periodically. That's it. Those four hours ensure your family doesn't spend four years in legal hell.

Don't wait. Don't postpone. Don't convince yourself you'll do it someday. This week, within the next seven days, do these five things.

Spend two to three hours creating your asset map. List every account, every investment, every asset. Use whatever format you will maintain. Don't aim for perfection, aim for completion.

Pick your largest investment—mutual fund, PF, insurance, and update the nomination if it's outdated. Set a reminder to update others systematically over the next month.

Identify your trusted guardian. Have a brief conversation: "I want you to know where my financial information is. Can we talk once a year to keep you updated?"

Google lawyers in your city who specialise in will writing, call two or three and ask for quotes. Or research online will platforms.

If you have physical share certificates, contact your broker and initiate dematerialisation. Don't wait for the perfect time. Start now.

Finally, set a recurring annual reminder on your calendar for your legacy planning review. Choose a meaningful date and commit to updating everything on that date every year.

Seven days. Each day requires 30 to 60 minutes. By next Sunday, you'll have more legacy planning done than 95% of Indians.

You've spent this entire book planning for your retirement—calculating expenses, building a corpus, managing investments, and optimising withdrawals. You've done the hard work of ensuring your money lasts through your lifetime. Now do the easy work of ensuring your money reaches the right people after your lifetime.

Not for your sake—you will be gone. For your family's sake. For your spouse who's grieving and shouldn't have to fight banks. For your children who should receive your legacy without years of legal battles. For the causes you care about that deserve your support even after you're gone.

Your life's work deserves a proper ending. Give it one.

You've built your Desi Retirement Plan. Now protect it with your legacy plan. Your family will thank you for it—even if they never have to use it. And that, ultimately, is the whole point.

25

Why Active Income Matters?

As you step into retirement, many people fall into the trap of thinking their income needs will decline, and it's time to stop working altogether. But what if I told you that this phase of life could be more financially enriching if you continue to generate active income and savings? Active income—whether through a part-time job, consulting, or gig work—ensures you remain in control of your financial destiny and keeps your skills sharp.

When we talk about active income in retirement, it's not about re-entering the grind or working 9 to 5. It's about finding meaningful ways to stay engaged, to make use of your experience, and to earn in a way that suits your lifestyle. And the good news is, there are numerous ways you can remain actively involved while still enjoying your retirement.

But there's another element that often gets overlooked in retirement planning: savings. It's easy to think that after working all those years, the savings phase is over. But it's not. You still need to save regularly—just like you did when you were building wealth during your working years. The magic of compounding is in full swing in retirement too, and the more you save, the more your wealth will continue to grow, even when you're not working full-time.

Exploring Gig Opportunities: Practical, Enjoyable Ways to Stay Active and Earn

You don't need to stop earning in retirement. With the rise of the gig economy, there are endless possibilities for retirees to stay engaged while bringing in extra income. Whether you want to work just a few hours a week or dedicate more time to a new passion, gigs allow you to stay involved without the pressure of a full-time job.

Here are 10 realistic gig opportunities for retirees in India:

1. Freelance Consulting

   Utilise your professional expertise in fields such as business, finance, marketing, or technology to consult for businesses or individuals. Consulting allows you to work at your own pace while earning a decent income.

2. Online Tutoring

   Several Online platforms offer retirees an excellent opportunity to teach, whether to school students or to professionals preparing for competitive exams.

3. Freelance Writing

   If you enjoy writing, consider starting a blog, writing articles, or doing content writing for websites. Even simple articles or short blogs can bring in a steady stream of income.

4. E-commerce (Selling Products Online)

   You can sell products on platforms like Amazon or Flipkart, whether they're handmade, vintage, or products that you've sourced from elsewhere.

5. Freelance Photography

   If you have a passion for photography, offer services for events like weddings or personal photo shoots, or sell stock photos online.

6. Event Planning

   Retirement is a time when you can organise and plan events at your own pace. Start small with family gatherings and gradually expand to weddings and corporate events.

7. Property Management

   Renting out property or managing other people's property can provide a reliable source of income. There are several online platforms that can help you list your property for short-term stays.

8. Yoga or Fitness Instructor

   If you're passionate about fitness, becoming a yoga or fitness instructor can be a great way to stay active and engaged while helping others.

9. Virtual Assistant

   Offer your administrative skills as a virtual assistant. You can help busy professionals manage their schedules, emails, and other tasks from the comfort of your home.

10. Transcription or Translation

    If you're bilingual, consider offering transcription or translation services. You can work from home and offer services to various businesses or platforms that need your skills.

HOW TO SELECT THE RIGHT GIG FOR YOU

Choosing the right gig involves balancing personal interests, skills, and the time commitment you're willing to make. Here are some tips for selecting the right gig:

What do I enjoy doing? If you love writing, start a blog or offer content creation services.

How much time do I want to invest? If you want to work a few hours a week, opt for gigs like online tutoring or freelance writing.

What are my skills? Leverage your career experience for consulting or mentoring.

What's the potential income? Consider the earning potential of different gigs—some may offer more income than others.

26

The Forever SIP: The One Habit You Never Break

I owe everything to one habit. Not a strategy, not a product, not a market call. A habit. Every financial goal I have ever reached—the home, my children's education, my retirement corpus traces back to a single decision I made early in my earning years: to invest a fixed amount every month, without fail, regardless of what the markets were doing. My SIP was not just an investment instruction. It was the discipline that built everything else.

So, when retirement finally arrived, the logical question presented itself: the goals are done, the corpus is built—should I not, finally, stop?

I sat with that question for a while. And the more I sat with it, the clearer the answer became.

My SIP does not end when I retire. It ends when I do. That is what forever means.

To discontinue my SIP would be to cut the one thread that runs through every phase of my financial life—from the first rupee I ever saved to the last one I will ever invest. I could not do it. And I believe that once you understand what continues to be possible, you will not want to, either.

This is the idea behind the Forever SIP.

WHY MUST THE HABIT CONTINUE?

In the previous chapter, we talked about the importance of staying active—of generating income through the early years of retirement. The Forever SIP is the natural companion to that income. Every rupee earned in retirement carries within it a choice: spend it entirely or save a part of it and put it to work.

The case for continuing to save is not complicated. It rests on one word: compounding. Your Desi Retirement Plan spans 30 to 35 years. Most people think of those years purely as a period of withdrawal. The Forever SIP asks a different question: what if a portion of those years was still spent building?

₹10,000 / month for 20 years @ 12% p.a. accumulates to ₹91 lakhs

Not magic. Just compounding, given time.

₹10,000 / month for 30 years @ 12% accumulates to ₹3.0 crore

Ten more years. More than three times the outcome.

The numbers are not projections designed to impress. They are simple arithmetic—the arithmetic of patience. What they illustrate is that the retirement years themselves, if used wisely, can produce wealth that rivals what you built during an entire career. Not by taking risks. By staying consistent.

HOW MUCH TO SET ASIDE?

During my working years, I followed two rules that I can take full credit for: I saved 10% of my take-home salary every month without exception, and I set aside 50% of every bonus before it could be spent. That was my mantra. It is what separates intention from result.

In retirement, the same spirit applies, adapted to the new reality. You no longer have a salary, but if you are generating active income, as we discussed in the previous chapter, you have something to work with.

The Forever SIP amount need not be large. I suggest starting with 5% of your monthly expenses.

Treat it as an expense. It comes out first, just as it always did. The lifestyle built on the remaining 95% is the lifestyle you live.

Do not underestimate what this seemingly small discipline can produce. Over 25 to 30 years, a Forever SIP has the potential to grow into a corpus that matches or exceeds the retirement corpus you spent your career building. Only this time, you are building it for the people who come after you.

THE POWER OF THE LONG RUN

Nobody knows exactly what returns the markets will deliver over the next three decades. That uncertainty is real, and it is honest to acknowledge it. But here is what we do know: saving regularly over a long period, in a disciplined and diversified manner, has never failed to create meaningful wealth across any 25-year period in Indian market history.

The table below shows what an investment of ₹1,000 can grow to over different time periods. Look at it not as a guarantee, but as a portrait of what patience makes possible.

Investment Returns (% p.a.)

Years	Savings	6%	8%	10%	12%
5	60,000	69,824	73,414	77,172	81,104
10	1,20,000	1,63,264	1,81,283	2,01,458	2,24,036
15	1,80,000	2,88,308	3,39,778	4,01,621	4,75,931
20	2,40,000	4,55,646	5,72,660	7,23,987	9,19,857
25	3,00,000	6,79,581	9,14,839	12,43,160	17,02,207
30	3,60,000	9,79,256	14,17,613	20,79,293	30,80,973
35	4,20,000	13,80,290	21,56,353	34,25,893	55,10,831
40	4,80,000	19,16,963	32,41,804	55,94,607	97,93,071

The lesson is the same regardless of which row you look at: no one who saved consistently and stayed invested for long enough ever looked back and wished they had saved less.

What is the Forever SIP really?

The Forever SIP is not a product. No fund house will sell it to you. It is a decision, a commitment you make to yourself that the habit that built your financial life will not be abandoned simply because the original goals have been met.

New goals emerge. Children get married. Grandchildren are born. Health needs arise that no plan fully anticipates. The world changes in ways that make a larger corpus always more useful than a smaller one.

And beyond the practical, there is something else. The act of saving, of investing, of building—it keeps you anchored to the future. It gives retirement a forward momentum that pure withdrawal never can. You are not just drawing down what you built. You are still building.

The Forever SIP is the one promise worth keeping for as long as you are alive to keep it.

Start with 5% of your expenses. If you can do 10%—that's even better. When active income stops, start saving from your withdrawals. Automate it so the decision does not have to be made each month. Choose any mutual fund, riskier the better! You are treating it as an expense, so in any case, you have written it off. And then do what you have always done best, leave it alone and let time do the rest.

The habit that built everything you have is still working. Do not be the one to stop it.

To conclude, Active Income and Regular Savings do matter as much in retirement as they did in your earning years. We are almost at the end of the Desi Retirement Plan, but I do not want a critical subject to be missed out—the Desi Retirement Plan for women. In the next chapter, you will find out why women should show interest in retirement planning even more than men and what is it that they need to know to be successful with their retirement planning.

27

Why Women Need to Plan Retirement Differently?

Women investors are unique, and one of the biggest reasons is something outside their control: women tend to live longer. And that changes everything.

In India, women typically marry men who are two to four years older. In earlier generations, that gap was often wider—five, six, sometimes eight years. Add to this the fact that women, on average, outlive men by three to five years. Current data suggests life expectancy for Indian women is around 71 years, versus 68 for men, and many women live well into their eighties and nineties. Now look at what this means in practice. If you marry someone three years older and outlive him by four years, you are likely to spend at least seven years managing life entirely on your own. If the age gap is wider, or if you live longer than average, this could extend to 10 or even 15 years.

That is not a short phase. That is a meaningful part of retirement, often the later years, when healthcare needs are higher, and every financial decision falls squarely on you—every investment choice, every withdrawal, every interaction with a bank, a mutual fund company, or a financial adviser. This is not a pessimistic view. It is simply an acknowledgement of reality. If anything, it is an opportunity to prepare, to build confidence, and to ensure that when the time comes, you are not starting from scratch.

The question is not whether you will face this phase. The question is: will you be ready for it?

FIVE REASONS RETIREMENT PLANNING IS DIFFERENT FOR WOMEN

Longevity is just one part of the story. There are four other factors that make retirement planning for women both more important and more nuanced. Taken together, they do not represent weaknesses. They represent realities—and once acknowledged, they can be addressed.

The first is career breaks. Many women step away from their careers at different stages—for childcare, eldercare, family responsibilities, or relocation. Each break is understandable. Each is often necessary. But financially, every break carries a cost that is easy to underestimate. A continuous 30-year career builds not just income but compounding. A career with breaks reduces both contributions and the time those contributions can grow. Missing even seven or eight years of savings can translate into a significantly smaller retirement corpus, not just because of the missed savings themselves, but because of the compounding those savings would have generated over the years that follow.

The second is the income gap. On average, women in India earn less than men for similar roles. Lower income means lower savings capacity, which directly reduces long-term wealth creation. This is not a fairness argument; it is a planning one. If your income is structurally lower, your savings rate and investment discipline need to be structurally higher to compensate. The plan must be built on reality, not on what the numbers ought to be.

The third is investment behaviour. Women tend to be more cautious investors, and in many ways, that is a genuine strength; it helps avoid reckless decisions and excessive risk-taking. But taken to an extreme, caution can become its own kind of risk. A portfolio earning 6%–7% in an environment where inflation runs at 5%–6% barely grows in real terms. Over long periods, the difference between cautious and well-balanced returns is not marginal; it is transformational. Consider: ₹1 crore growing at 7% per annum becomes approximately ₹7.6 crores over 30 years. At 9%, it becomes ₹13.3 crores. That difference, nearly ₹6 crores from a 2% improvement in annual returns, is the cost of excessive caution.

The fourth is the pattern of prioritising others over oneself. Education, family needs, a spouse's business, emergencies—women frequently put their own financial goals second. Each individual decision is generous. Often necessary. Sometimes both. But over time, the cumulative effect of consistently deferring your own financial planning is a retirement that is underfunded precisely when it needs to be most secure.

The fifth is limited involvement in financial decisions. In many households, one person manages the finances, often the husband. The arrangement works smoothly for years, sometimes decades. But when circumstances change through death, illness, divorce, or simply the natural passage of time, the transition can be abrupt. The challenge is not a lack of ability. It is a lack of familiarity. The accounts exist, the investments are in place, but the knowledge of where things are and how to operate them has never been built. That gap, when it matters most, is the hardest one to close quickly.

WHAT YOU NEED TO KNOW AND HOW TO BUILD IT

You do not need to become a financial expert. You do not need to track markets daily or master complex products. What you need is comfort with the basics, and that comfort is built through familiarity, not study. The goal is not to understand everything. The goal is to be able to act when it matters.

Start with your banking. Know how to check your balance, transfer money, pay bills, open and close fixed deposits, and read a bank statement. Know what to do if something goes wrong and who to call. This is the foundation, not because it is the most important thing, but because it is the most immediate and most frequently used. Once it feels routine, it stops feeling difficult.

Move from there to your investments. Know where your mutual funds are held, how to log in to the platform, how to view your portfolio, and how to redeem units if you need to. If you have a demat account, understand how to see your holdings and place a basic transaction. You do not need to manage the portfolio actively. You need to be able to access it, understand what you own, and act if circumstances require it. The same applies to insurance policies, fixed deposits, and any other financial instruments in your name or jointly held.

Know your documents and where they are. Account statements, insurance policies, property papers, and identification documents—can you access them when needed? Create a simple, clear list of your assets. Not in someone else's head. Not in scattered papers. But in your own understanding, written down, and updated regularly. This single step, "the asset list", is one of the most practically valuable things you can do for your future self.

Know your people. Who is your financial adviser? Your chartered accountant? Your banker? Have you spoken to them directly, not through a spouse or family member? Build relationships with these individuals now, not after a crisis makes it necessary. And identify one person—an adviser, a knowledgeable friend, a trusted family member who will speak to you clearly, explain things in plain language, and not rush you towards decisions you do not yet understand.

BUILDING COMPETENCE WITHOUT FEELING OVERWHELMED

The key is one step at a time, with no rush and no judgement. Begin with your bank account. Log in. Explore the interface. Transfer a small amount to yourself. Pay a bill. Repeat until it feels unremarkable. Once it does, move to your mutual fund platform. Log in, look at your portfolio, and understand what each fund is. No need to take any action, simply observe. Then move to your demat account if you have one, and do the same.

At the same time, work on your asset list. Write down what you own in plain language—which bank accounts, which mutual funds, which insurance policies, which properties. Note where the documents are. Update it once every six months. This list is not for anyone else. It is for you so that you always know where you stand and, if circumstances change, you or someone you trust can act quickly and clearly.

Use whatever learning resources work for you—videos, articles, tutorials, conversations. Pause, repeat, revisit. There is no syllabus and no deadline. Learn with others if possible: many women are on the same journey, and shared learning reduces the sense of isolation that financial unfamiliarity can create. Practice with small amounts. Make your early mistakes where they do not matter. Build the muscle gradually, and do not wait for the perfect moment to begin.

A practical structure that many women find useful is a three-month sprint to build basic financial independence. The first month focused on banking—logging in daily, transferring small amounts, and reading statements. The second month on investments, reviewing the portfolio, understanding what is owned, and creating the asset summary. The third month is spent on building the support system, identifying trusted advisers, organising documents, and completing the asset map. After those three months, one new skill or task per month is enough. Within a year, you will not be an expert. But you will be comfortable. And in financial life, comfort is what makes you act.

Beyond Skills: Building Confidence

Knowledge matters, but confidence is what makes you act on it. And confidence in financial matters is built the same way it is built in any other domain—through small decisions made repeatedly until they no longer feel uncertain. Start making decisions, even minor ones. Increase an SIP. Choose where to place a fixed deposit. Review an insurance policy and decide whether to renew it. Not every decision needs to be perfect. Mistakes will happen, and that is part of the process. What matters is that you remain engaged rather than delegating decisions you are fully capable of making yourself.

Learn to pause before decisions that feel urgent but are not. A good financial decision made in three days is almost always better than a rushed one made in three hours. Seek advice when you need it; that is not a sign of weakness, it is a sign of judgement. And recognise what you already bring to this. You have managed a household, balanced competing priorities, handled uncertainty, and made consequential decisions for years. Those skills—the capacity to plan, to allocate resources, to think about others' needs alongside your own, to remain steady under pressure—translate directly and powerfully into financial decision-making. You are not starting from zero.

FOR SINGLE WOMEN AND WIDOWS

If you are already managing your finances independently—whether by choice, circumstance, or necessity, you are further ahead than you may realise. You have direct experience with decisions that many women are only beginning to encounter. You may still have gaps in knowledge or confidence, but you also have something that cannot be taught quickly: the experience of having made decisions and lived with their consequences.

The priorities for women managing independently are straightforward. Build a larger emergency fund than the standard guidance suggests—three months of expenses is the conventional advice, but for a single person without a second income to fall back on, six months is a more prudent target. Keep your documentation clear, current, and accessible. Make sure at least one trusted person knows where things are and has the access needed to help in an emergency. Stay connected to your advisers and update them when your circumstances change. Independence is not about doing everything alone. It is about knowing clearly what you own, what you owe, and when and how to seek support.

A NOTE TO THE MEN IN THE HOUSEHOLD

If you are reading this, and I hope many men are, this matters more than most financial decisions you will make. The greatest gift you can give the women in your life is not just wealth but the ability to manage it. Involve them in financial decisions, not as observers but as participants. Explain things. Share access to accounts and platforms. Encourage direct relationships with advisers, bankers, and accountants. Make joint financial reviews a regular part of your household, not something that happens only when something goes wrong.

This is not about anticipating the worst. It is about acknowledging that life is unpredictable, and that preparation is not a response to fear; it is an expression of responsibility. The financial knowledge and familiarity that you have built over the years cannot be transferred in a crisis. It can only be built gradually, through participation and practice. Give the people you love the time and the environment to build it.

This chapter is not about capability. Women are more than capable of managing money, often with greater discipline, patience, and clarity than their male counterparts. What is sometimes missing is exposure and practice. And both of those can be built, at any age, starting from wherever you are today.

You have already spent time working through this book, understanding your retirement expenses, your investment options, your risk profile, and your withdrawal strategy. You have the framework. This chapter is simply about ensuring that when the time comes to act on that framework, you can do so with confidence and independence rather than uncertainty and dependence.

Your financial future is ultimately your responsibility. Not because others will not help; they will, but because you are the one constant in your own life. Your retirement is not just something you plan for; it is something you will live. And that requires not just wealth but the ability to manage it. Build both.

28

Your Desi Retirement Preparedness Score

You have done more thinking about your retirement than most people ever will. You have thought about your responsibilities, estimated your expenses, examined your investments, and calculated your AWR. At this point, the natural question is simple: am I ready?

The honest answer is that no single number answers it completely. Retirement preparedness is not just about returns or corpus size. It is about how well the entire plan holds together, whether the pieces connect, whether the assumptions are realistic, and whether you have genuinely thought through the dimensions that matter most.

The Desi Retirement Preparedness Score, or DRPS, was designed precisely for this. It gives you one more opportunity, structured and comprehensive, to assess where you stand. Even those who find numbers difficult will find this assessment straightforward. What it asks for is not calculation but honest reflection.

Score	What it means
1	Not in place - you are not prepared at all
2	Weakly in place - you have started thinking about it
3	Partially in place - you are somewhat ready
4	Mostly in place - a few gaps remain
5	Strong and well thought through - you are fully in control

THE DESI RETIREMENT PREPAREDNESS SCORECARD

Questions 01 – 10

1 = Not in place   2 = Weakly   3 = Partial   4 = Mostly   5 = Fully in place

01 PEOPLE CLARITY
Do I have a complete and honest picture of everyone who depends on me? ____/5

02 PROMISES PLANNED
Have I identified and provided for all major commitments — for myself and my core circle? ____/5

03 LONGEVITY AWARENESS
Am I financially prepared to meet my expenses until age 100? ____/5

04 EXPENSE REALISM
Do I have a realistic and comprehensive estimate of my retirement lifestyle expenses? ____/5

05 HEALTHCARE READINESS
Am I prepared for medical realities — with insurance, a buffer, and emergency liquidity? ____/5

06 INFLATION AWARENESS
Have I accounted for how my expenses will grow over the next 10, 20, and 30 years? ____/5

07 INCOME VISIBILITY
Do I clearly know how my expenses will be funded each year in retirement? ____/5

08 INVESTMENT CORPUS
Do I have an accurate and complete view of my total investment corpus? ____/5

09 RETIREMENT CORPUS
Have I correctly separated what is available for retirement from what is already committed? ____/5

10 WITHDRAWAL RATE
Is my Annual Withdrawal Rate at a level I can sustain with confidence? ____/5

THE DESI RETIREMENT PREPAREDNESS SCORECARD

Questions 11 – 20
1 = Not in place 2 = Weakly 3 = Partial 4 = Mostly 5 = Fully in place
Add all 20 scores for your total DRPS out of 100

11 ACTION ORIENTATION
Am I actively taking steps to improve my retirement preparedness? ____/5

12 BEHAVIOURAL BIASES
Am I aware of the investment biases that may affect my financial decisions? ____/5

13 RETURN ASSUMPTIONS
Have I made realistic assumptions about the returns my investments will generate? ____/5

14 DIVERSIFICATION
Is my portfolio genuinely diversified across debt, equity, gold, and real estate? ____/5

15 TAXATION
Do I understand the tax implications when I liquidate my investments? ____/5

16 PRODUCT KNOWLEDGE
Do I understand the key products I will invest in during retirement? ____/5

17 STRESS TEST
Have I tested my plan against adverse scenarios — lower returns, higher inflation, market downturns? ____/5

18 DRAWDOWN STRATEGY
Do I have a clear plan for how and in what sequence I will draw down my corpus? ____/5

19 LEGACY READINESS
Have I ensured clarity for my family through documentation, nominations, and a will? ____/5

20 REVIEW DISCIPLINE
Am I clear about how often I need to review my retirement plan — and do I actually do it? ____/5

YOUR DRPS SCORE

Add up your scores for all 20 questions:

Total Score: _____/100

How to interpret your score:

Your DRPS	Zone	What it means
80 – 100	Strong Control	You are well prepared. Focus on consistency and refinement.
60 – 79	Progress in Motion	You are on the right path. Some gaps need structured attention.
40 – 59	Fragile Plan	Your plan needs strengthening. Prioritise the lowest-scoring areas immediately.
Below 40	At Risk	Your plan is based on assumptions. It is time to take structured action.

Where are my biggest gaps?

____

____

____

What is the one action I will take immediately?

____

____

____

When will I review this scorecard next?

____

____

____

Your Desi Retirement Preparedness Score is not a judgement. It is your starting point—and your roadmap back to the chapters that will move your score forward.

Conclusion – My Rules for Retirement

Let me begin by saying that the purpose of writing this book was simple—to help you build a retirement plan that works for you and is grounded in the realities we face in India.

Retirement is a complex subject. Despite my best efforts, there will always be areas that I may not have covered. But if this book has helped you ask the right questions, and if you now have a broad sketch of what your retirement could look like, I will consider that a meaningful outcome.

As we come to the end, let me leave you with five simple rules for a fulfilling retirement. These are not theoretical ideas—they are principles that have worked for me and can serve as a guide for you as well.

RULE #1: STAY HEALTHY

You do not need the fitness of an athlete. What matters is consistency—the ability to take care of yourself day after day. Adequate sleep, moderation in diet, and some form of regular exercise go a long way. It sounds simple, but it is often the hardest to follow.

RULE #2: STAY CONNECTED

Retirement is not just about financial independence—it is also about emotional well-being. Spend time with family and friends. Nurture the relationships that matter. In the end, these are what give meaning to your time.

RULE #3: LIVE LIFE ON YOUR TERMS

During your working years, you often must compromise on time, priorities, and sometimes even choices. Retirement gives you the opportunity to reclaim that freedom. Use it well. Design your life in a way that reflects what truly matters to you.

RULE #4: HAVE A RETIREMENT PLAN

A plan does not have to be perfect. In fact, it rarely is. But having a plan keeps you anchored—it helps you stay aligned with your financial reality and better prepared for uncertainties. The goal is not perfection, but direction.

RULE #5: STAY DIVERSIFIED IN INVESTING

Investment success is not about chasing the best-performing asset. It is about managing risk and staying balanced. Diversification helps you move beyond personal biases and build a portfolio that can withstand different market conditions.

Retirement is a long journey. There will be changes, surprises, and adjustments along the way. But with clarity, preparation, and the right mindset, it can also be one of the most rewarding phases of your life.

I wish you and your family the very best in life!

About the Author

Suraj Kaeley is a distinguished senior leader in the financial services sector, with an extensive track record of leadership across prominent organisations.

He started his career with HDFC Ltd. in 1988 as a Management Trainee. His career includes key roles at Franklin Templeton India Asset Management, MetLife India Insurance, and FIL Fund Management (a division of Fidelity Worldwide), where he contributed to the growth and success of these institutions within the Indian market. In his last corporate role, he served as Group President—Sales & Marketing at UTI Asset Management, where he was instrumental in shaping the company's sales strategies and driving innovative marketing initiatives, significantly enhancing client engagement and business growth.

He currently mentors his son, who founded Ortium Financial Services Private Limited, a mutual fund distribution firm based out of Mumbai.

He is very passionate about investing and has worked relentlessly to popularise the concept of SIP investing in the country.

Annexure I

EXPENSE HEADS

MONTHLY ESSENTIAL

Personal Consumption: Groceries, toiletries, cosmetics, spa and salon

Utilities / House help: Electricity, gas, telephone, Wi-Fi, OTT subscriptions, house help, drivers

Local Travel: Petrol, diesel, PNG, tolls, taxi services

MONTHLY DESIRABLE

Personal Lifestyle: Cosmetics, spa and salon, clothing and accessories, footwear

Entertainment: Dining out, takeaway, delivery to home, movies, theatre

ANNUAL

Insurance premiums (life, health, vehicles, HH)

Property taxes/maintenance

Vacations (domestic and international)

Education fees

Taxes and subscriptions

PERIODIC EXPENSES (ONCE IN A FEW YEARS)

Household effects (furniture and fixtures, painting, white goods, art décor, etc.), vehicle replacement

Annexure II

FUTURE VALUE OF ₹1

Future Value of ₹ 1

Year	4%	5%	6%	7%	8%	9%	10%	11%	12%
1	1.04	1.05	1.06	1.07	1.08	1.09	1.10	1.11	1.12
2	1.08	1.10	1.12	1.14	1.17	1.19	1.21	1.23	1.25
3	1.12	1.16	1.19	1.23	1.26	1.30	1.33	1.37	1.40
4	1.17	1.22	1.26	1.31	1.36	1.41	1.46	1.52	1.57
5	1.22	1.28	1.34	1.40	1.47	1.54	1.61	1.69	1.76
6	1.27	1.34	1.42	1.50	1.59	1.68	1.77	1.87	1.97
7	1.32	1.41	1.50	1.61	1.71	1.83	1.95	2.08	2.21
8	1.37	1.48	1.59	1.72	1.85	1.99	2.14	2.30	2.48
9	1.42	1.55	1.69	1.84	2.00	2.17	2.36	2.56	2.77
10	1.48	1.63	1.79	1.97	2.16	2.37	2.59	2.84	3.11
11	1.54	1.71	1.90	2.10	2.33	2.58	2.85	3.15	3.48
12	1.60	1.80	2.01	2.25	2.52	2.81	3.14	3.50	3.90
13	1.67	1.89	2.13	2.41	2.72	3.07	3.45	3.88	4.36
14	1.73	1.98	2.26	2.58	2.94	3.34	3.80	4.31	4.89
15	1.80	2.08	2.40	2.76	3.17	3.64	4.18	4.78	5.47
16	1.87	2.18	2.54	2.95	3.43	3.97	4.59	5.31	6.13
17	1.95	2.29	2.69	3.16	3.70	4.33	5.05	5.90	6.87
18	2.03	2.41	2.85	3.38	4.00	4.72	5.56	6.54	7.69
19	2.11	2.53	3.03	3.62	4.32	5.14	6.12	7.26	8.61
20	2.19	2.65	3.21	3.87	4.66	5.60	6.73	8.06	9.65
25	2.67	3.39	4.29	5.43	6.85	8.62	10.83	13.59	17.00
30	3.24	4.32	5.74	7.61	10.06	13.27	17.45	22.89	29.96
35	3.95	5.52	7.69	10.68	14.79	20.41	28.10	38.57	52.80
40	4.80	7.04	10.29	14.97	21.72	31.41	45.26	65.00	93.05

This table can help you with the calculation of (a) the impact of inflation and (b) the growth of your lump-sum investments.

For example, anything that costs ₹1 today will cost ₹10.29 after 40 years @ inflation rate of 6% p.a. (look up at the intersection of row 40 years and rate 6% p.a. for the relevant number)

So, if your monthly expense is ₹50,000 at today's value, the same goods and services will cost you 50,000 multiplied by 10.29 = ₹514,500 after 40 years (assuming inflation @ 6% p.a.)

You can also calculate the future value of your investments using this table.

For example, if you invest ₹50,000 and earn a return of 6% p.a. for 40 years, your investment will grow to ₹514,500. (50,000 multiplied by 10.29)

Annexure III

FUTURE VALUE OF INVESTING ₹1 PER MONTH

Future Value of investing ₹ 1 per month

Years	6%	7%	8%	9%	10%	11%	12%
1	12.39	12.45	12.51	12.58	12.64	12.70	12.77
2	25.52	25.77	26.03	26.29	26.55	26.80	27.06
3	39.43	40.03	40.63	41.23	41.84	42.46	43.08
4	54.19	55.28	56.39	57.52	58.66	59.83	61.02
5	69.82	71.59	73.41	75.27	77.17	79.12	81.18
6	86.40	89.06	91.80	94.62	97.53	100.52	103.60
7	103.97	107.75	111.66	115.72	119.92	124.28	128.80
8	122.60	127.74	133.11	138.71	144.56	150.65	157.02
9	142.34	149.13	156.27	163.77	171.65	179.93	188.63
10	163.25	172.02	181.28	191.09	201.46	212.43	224.04
11	185.45	196.51	208.30	220.86	234.24	248.50	263.69
12	208.95	222.72	237.48	253.32	270.31	288.54	308.10
13	233.88	250.76	268.99	288.59	309.98	332.98	357.83
14	260.30	280.76	303.02	327.25	353.62	382.31	413.54
15	288.31	312.86	339.78	369.28	401.62	437.07	475.93
16	317.99	347.21	379.47	415.09	454.42	497.85	545.81
17	349.46	383.97	422.35	466.03	512.51	565.32	624.07
18	382.81	423.38	468.65	519.46	576.48	649.21	711.73
19	418.17	465.38	518.65	578.79	646.58	723.34	809.90
20	455.65	510.41	572.66	643.46	723.99	815.61	919.85
25	679.58	787.47	914.84	1,065.31	1,243.16	1,453.46	1,702.21
30	979.25	1,176.95	1,417.61	1,714.38	2,079.29	2,528.28	3,080.97
35	1,380.29	1,721.09	2,156.35	2,713.06	3,425.89	4,339.42	5,510.83
40	1,916.96	2,485.52	3,241.80	4,249.65	5,594.61	7,391.29	9,793.07

Many of you must be investing in Systematic Investment Plans (SIPs). If you want to know how much your SIP investment will grow over time, the above table can help you compute that number with ease.

For example, ₹1 invested for 40 years @ 12% p.a. will grow to ₹9793.07. (This number is at the intersection of row 40 years and investment return of 12% p.a.—the bottom corner of the above table).

Imagine what would happen if you decided to save ₹10,000 per month for 40 years and you earn 12% p.a. on your investments. Your investments will grow to ₹9,79,30,700—yes, you read it right, almost ₹10 Crores. This is the magic of compounding. Albert Einstein termed it the 8th wonder of the world.

You can also use this table to determine the monthly savings that you need to make to achieve a particular targeted sum.

Let's take the above example. You wanted to create a wealth of ₹10 Crores in your lifetime (in 40 years), and you expect to earn about 12% p.a. on your investments. All you need to do is divide 10,00,00,000 by 9793.07 (the same factor that we used in the earlier example). The answer is what you will need to save monthly. This number works out to 10,211. If you save ₹10,211 every month and earn 12% p.a., your savings will grow to ₹10 Crores! Wow!

www.ingramcontent.com/pod-product-compliance
Lightning Source LLC
LaVergne TN
LVHW100302210926
848480LV00003B/1000
* 9 7 9 8 9 0 4 3 1 3 5 6 2 *